"Linda Matias, an expert in candidate coaching for interview success, provides a veritable encyclopedia in her latest book, *How to Say It: Job Interviews.* She dispels many common myths and provides exceptionally practical how-tos with both a strategy and a plan for effective execution. There are numerous scripts interspersed between nuggets of value designed to help everyone (from the recent college graduate to the seasoned executive) ace the interview."

—Jan Melnik, MRW, CCM, CPRW, coauthor of
Executive's Pocket Guide to ROI Resumes and Job Search

"*How to Say It: Job Interviews* offers a thorough listing of power words and phrases for the pre-interview, interview, and post-interview process. . . . Both experienced jobseekers and those new to the workforce will find sound interview advice in this book."

—Maurene J. Hinds, author of
The Ferguson Guide to Resumes and Job-Hunting Skills

"*How to Say It: Job Interviews* offers a pragmatic guide for applicants to use in preparing for job interviews. From developing good references to adapting to different interview scenarios and, ultimately, negotiating a favorable compensation package, this book offers easy-to-follow, sound advice for job seekers."

—Arnie Boldt, CPRW, JCTC, coauthor of
No-Nonsense Resumes and *No-Nonsense Cover Letters*

continued . . .

"Job interview guru Linda Matias provides refreshing strategies for nailing the interview in her excellent book, *How to Say It: Job Interviews.* Matias teaches the reader how to adapt to various interview styles and offers a comprehensive list of answers to common interview questions. Chock-full of practical and effective advice, Matias's book is a must-read for job seekers who are serious about acing the interview."

—Kim Isaacs, author of *The Career Change Resume;*
director of ResumePower.com; and
Monster.com's Resume Expert

"*How to Say It: Job Interviews* truly stands out from similar career guides. Linda Matias demystifies the employment interview process through her reader-friendly delivery of proven strategies, techniques, and sample 'How to Say It' scripts for virtually every interview situation and career field."

—Murray A. Mann, author of Barron's
The Complete Job Search Guide for Latinos

HOW TO SAY IT

Job Interviews

Linda Matias,
JCTC, CIC, NCRW

PRENTICE HALL PRESS

PRENTICE HALL PRESS
Published by the Penguin Group
Penguin Group (USA) Inc.
375 Hudson Street, New York, New York 10014, USA
Penguin Group (Canada), 90 Eglinton Avenue East, Suite 700, Toronto, Ontario M4P 2Y3, Canada
(a division of Pearson Penguin Canada Inc.)
Penguin Books Ltd., 80 Strand, London WC2R 0RL, England
Penguin Group Ireland, 25 St. Stephen's Green, Dublin 2, Ireland (a division of Penguin Books Ltd.)
Penguin Group (Australia), 250 Camberwell Road, Camberwell, Victoria 3124, Australia
(a division of Pearson Australia Group Pty. Ltd.)
Penguin Books India Pvt. Ltd., 11 Community Centre, Panchsheel Park, New Delhi—110 017, India
Penguin Group (NZ), 67 Apollo Drive, Rosedale, North Shore 0632, New Zealand
(a division of Pearson New Zealand Ltd.)
Penguin Books (South Africa) (Pty.) Ltd., 24 Sturdee Avenue, Rosebank, Johannesburg 2196,
South Africa

Penguin Books Ltd., Registered Offices: 80 Strand, London WC2R 0RL, England

Cover art by Paul Howalt
Cover design by Ben Gibson
Text design by Tiffany Estreicher

First edition: August 2007

Library of Congress Cataloging-in-Publication Data

Matias, Linda.
How to say it : job interviews / Linda Matias. — 1st ed.
p. cm.
Includes bibliographical references and index.
ISBN 978-0-7352-0422-5
1. Employment interviewing—Handbooks, manuals, etc. 2. Job hunting—Handbooks, manuals, etc. I. Title.
HF5549.5.I6M318 2007
650.14'4—dc22

2007009371

PRINTED IN THE UNITED STATES OF AMERICA

10 9 8 7 6 5 4 3

To my big sister, Bobbi, who has always believed in me

and

my first grade teacher, Mrs. Picozzi, who taught me
my greatest life lesson—the tremendous power of empathy.

Acknowledgments

Many of the responses included in this book are from real-life examples taken from coaching sessions I've had with clients throughout the years. I'd like to thank each and every one of them for sharing their interview experiences with me and allowing me to be part of their job searches.

As the facilitator for the Certified Interview Coach designation, I'd like to acknowledge all the students and graduates of the institute for their dedication to the career services industry. I've had the pleasure not only of teaching them the ins and outs of interview coaching, but also of having the opportunity to learn from them.

In addition, I'd like to recognize Dan Dorotik for being an outstanding wordsmith, John Collado for his unwavering support of my endeavors, and HR representatives and hiring managers who shared their insights with me.

I also want to thank my editor, Maria Gagliano, whose thoughts and ideas were instrumental in shaping the final outcome of this book. And most especially, I want to thank my agent, Barret Neville, for his continued support and encouragement.

Contents

Introduction

How to Say It: Job Interviews will provide you with the tools, words, phrases, and scripts needed to shine in all phases of the interview. From that ever-so-important first impression through all the stages of the interview process through effective follow-up strategies, *How to Say It: Job Interviews* will empower you to approach the interview process with confidence in your ability to "work" the interview room and communicate your goals and accomplishments.

COMMON INTERVIEW MYTHS

Throughout my years as an interview coach, I noticed that both recent college graduates and seasoned executives use the same tired technique: They show up the day of the interview without much preparation, holding on to the following interview myths that hinder their ability to land positions.

- ***Myth 1: The interview begins when I'm sitting across from the interviewer.*** Many job seekers believe the time to start making an impression is when they are invited in for an interview.

Truth: The interview process begins when you decide to search for a position. For the one-on-one meeting to go smoothly, you have a responsibility to learn how your skills, knowledge, and abilities are marketable. Simultaneously, you must be able to tie in what you offer to the needs of hiring organizations.

- ***Myth 2: The interviewer controls the interview.*** On the surface, this premise makes sense. The hiring organization is the one that is hiring, so it should have full control over what happens during an interview.

  Truth: Both you and the interviewer have a very specific role during the interview. Active participation from both sides will turn a ho-hum interview into a winning one. Let's take a look at the chart below.

Your Role in the Process	The Interviewer's Role in the Process
Elaborate on the information provided in the résumé and help the interviewer connect the dots between your skills and knowledge and see how each relates to the open position	Assess the candidate's abilities and verify if the résumé represents what the candidate has to offer

Demonstrate a strong work ethic and the know-how to exceed organizational goals	Determine if the candidate is willing and able to implement the requirements set forth in the job description
Understand the corporate culture and determine whether your personality complements the organization's work style and expectations	Ensure the candidate's personal and work styles meet the cultural needs of the organization, coworkers, business associates, and vendors
Prove you are the best candidate for the position by answering each question with confidence and clarity	Ask questions that uncover the candidate's interest in working for the organization
Learn more about the organization, its products and services, clients, and the people it employs by asking questions throughout the interview	Openly answer questions posed so that candidates can make an educated decision on whether the organization is the right fit for them

As illustrated in the chart, your role and that of the interviewer overlap, and you both have responsibilities to ensure the interview goes smoothly.

- ***Myth 3: If the résumé is written correctly, it will reveal my qualifications.*** "See my résumé" is the common response given by candidates who are not prepared to answer interview questions.

Truth: The purpose of the résumé is to attract the attention of a hiring manager, but it is up to you to sell yourself during an interview and back up, as well as elaborate on, the information provided in the résumé.

Through sharpening your interview skills, you will be able to overcome these misconceptions and positively affect the outcome of the interview. When fully prepared, you will be equipped to handle yourself with poise, answer interview questions with ease, and articulately present your strengths.

How to Say It: Job Interviews will provide you with fundamental interviewing principles, thought-provoking preinterview exercises, sample interview answers, scripts, and interview-related letters you can draw on to improve your interview skills and land a job offer. The book is split into four parts to ensure that every aspect of the interview process is covered.

PART I: YOUR INTERVIEW TOOLKIT

Part I focuses on activities you can do to prepare for an interview and gives pointers you can use to perform well during interviews. You will learn how to craft a thirty-second pitch that demonstrates the immediate contributions you can bring to a hiring organization; how to coach your references to provide compelling statements on your behalf; and how to make a positive impression during interviews by dressing appropriately, becoming aware of your nonverbal communication, and overcoming anxiety.

PART II: ADAPTING TO DIFFERENT INTERVIEW FORMATS AND INTERVIEWER STYLES

Part II discusses how you can cultivate a strong network base that you can call on when participating in informational interviews. You'll learn about the types of interview formats you can expect to encounter and how to adapt your communication style to accommodate different interviewer personalities and organization cultures.

PART III: WINNING ANSWERS TO THE MOST COMMON INTERVIEW QUESTIONS

Part III shows you how to anticipate interview questions; provides sample interview questions you may be asked; offers a set of instructions you can follow to answer each question; and provides strategic instructions you can use to model your own responses. The sample questions compiled here come from professionals I know in the human resources industry who provided me with insight on the types of questions they ask and why. Others come from clients I've coached who shared the types of questions they've been asked by potential employers.

Whether you are new to the job market or a seasoned professional, the sample interview questions and answers provided in this book will apply. When needed, I include more than one response to the questions to accommodate a variety of job seekers.

PART IV: THE FINISH LINE

Part IV focuses on the importance of your asking questions during interviews and provides samples you can ask. I walk you through the process of effectively managing the negotiations process; provide sample scripts for how you can respond to questions regarding compensation and other benefits; and teach you how to effectively follow up with an interviewer by providing samples of thank-you, offer, and acceptance letters.

POWER WORDS, CHARACTERISTICS, AND POWER PHRASES

To make it easier for you to develop your own scripts, answers to interview questions, and interview-related letters, each chapter contains a list of power words, characteristics, and/or phrases you can use to help you get your message across. Integrating these power words, characteristics, and power phrases will help you describe the skills, experience, and strengths you have to offer to a hiring organization.

EXTRA HELP ONLINE

Once you have finished reading *How to Say It: Job Interviews* visit www.howtosayitjobinterviews.com. There you will find additional interview articles that will supplement the information in this book and podcasts you can download for your mp3 player so you can listen to advice on your way to an interview. The website is a great resource that will surely ease your interview jitters and provide last-minute interview tips that can make the difference on whether you receive a job offer. You can also subscribe to our free online newsletter and receive the latest interview trends directly to your inbox. In addition, you can share your interview success stories and the interview tips that have worked for you.

Your Interview Toolkit

1

Scoring Winning References

Interviewers conduct background and reference checks to verify the information you provide in your résumé and during the interview. If employers uncover red flags or inconsistencies during the reference-checking process that put your work performance, character, and trustworthiness into question your candidacy may be eliminated. For this reason, it is important that you choose credible references who (1) will speak enthusiastically on your behalf, (2) will provide a fair and balanced representation of your qualifications, (3) and have intimate knowledge of your experience and accomplishments.

This chapter will walk you through how to choose references and how you can approach each to vouch for your experience. References can range from human resource (HR) representatives, direct mangers, or colleagues to vendors, business associates, or recent professors. Employers craft different sets of reference questions depending on whom they are contacting. Lists of sample questions your references may be asked by a prospective employer follow.

Human Resource Representative

1. Why did the candidate leave the company?
2. How is the candidate's attendance record?
3. Has the candidate ever been promoted?
4. Is the candidate eligible for rehire?
5. Do you have any additional information or comments regarding the applicant that I should know?

Colleagues

1. Describe a project you recently worked on with the applicant. What was your role? His role? What was the end result?
2. Give an example of a time when the applicant emerged as a leader when working on a specific task. How did the applicant get cooperation from her coworkers?
3. Tell me about a time when the applicant worked effectively as a member of a team. How successful was the group in completing the task?
4. Tell me about a conflict you had with the applicant when working on a project. What was the conflict and how was it resolved?
5. In your opinion, does the applicant perform better in a team or individual environment?

Managers

1. This position requires strong customer-service skills. Can you describe how the applicant handles irate customers?
2. Can you tell me about a time when the applicant had to meet a tight deadline and was working against obstacles?

3. How would you describe the applicant's team-management skills?
4. In the applicant's last review, what did you say needed improvement?
5. Tell me about a high-pressure situation the applicant was in recently. How did he cope?

Direct Reports

1. How would you describe the applicant's management style?
2. What qualities do you feel make the applicant a successful manager?
3. Where do you disagree with the applicant most often?
4. What type of employee is most difficult for the applicant to manage?
5. How does the applicant's management style compare to other managers you've had?

Associates or Vendors

1. Did the applicant fulfill your project(s) on time, on budget, and to your complete satisfaction?
2. Did the applicant work collaboratively with you when defining and finalizing the scope of your needs?
3. How would you describe the applicant's ability to anticipate your concerns?
4. Did the applicant serve as an effective liaison when planning, organizing, directing, and coordinating project related activities?
5. How would you describe the applicant's negotiation style?

Because it is difficult to determine the exact questions that an interviewer will ask references, the lists can be used in two ways. Depending on the type of information you believe may be of interest to the interviewer, you can use the questions I provided as a guide to choose your references. You can also supply your references with the lists of questions so that they can prepare for the type of questions they may be asked.

APPROACHING SOMEONE FOR A REFERENCE

To avoid uncomfortable situations and word leaking that you are searching for new employment, refrain from approaching current employers, coworkers, business associates, and vendors for a reference. Instead, choose individuals that you had a good working relationship with in the past—doing so you will ensure that your confidentiality is maintained.

To make certain you'll receive proper and professional recommendations you should approach references well in advance. Failing to contact your references beforehand can lead to the following problems:

1. E-mail and physical addresses and phone numbers change over time. You want to make sure that you are giving potential employers the right contact information for your references. Supplying an interviewer with incorrect information will work against you. At worst, interviewers may assume that you provided false information purposely because you couldn't find someone to vouch for you. At best, they will believe you aren't taking your job

search seriously. In either scenario, you are giving the interviewer a valid reason to eliminate your candidacy.

2. Although you may vividly remember your working relationship with your references, they may need a gentle reminder. An unfortunate circumstance would ensue if your reference said, "*Who? Oh yeah yeah. I vaguely remember him. We used to work together at ABC Company, right? No? Where? Oh, that's right. He's a great guy. What would you like to know?*" when called for a reference. Approaching your references in advance will give you the opportunity to refresh their memories.
3. Although you may have fond memories of working with possible references, they may have a different recollection. Talking to your references ahead of time gives you the opportunity to determine if they are comfortable speaking on your behalf.

HOW TO HANDLE REFERENCE REQUESTS ON AN APPLICATION

Many job applications ask if the hiring organization can contact your current employer. If you don't want your current employer to know you are looking for another position and prefer to have the interviewer call after a firm offer has been made and accepted, make note of that on the application by simply writing, "At this time, please do not contact my current employer. Should an offer be extended and accepted, then you can feel free to do so."

Interviewers understand the sensitivity of the situation and will abide by your request. On the rare occasion that a potential employer insists on speaking to your current employer without a firm offer of employment, you must weigh your options carefully. The moment your current employer is aware you are looking to leave, he may decide it's best for you to clear out your desk immediately—leaving you without a job. Or he may not ask for your resignation but instead brand you a disloyal employee.

If you're confident that your current employer will be supportive of your decision to seek employment elsewhere, it's best to discuss whether he would be willing to give you a reference before providing contact information to a potential employer. One way to approach the conversation is by saying something along the lines of: *"Rachel, I have learned a lot from working with you and I have enjoyed my time here at ABC Company. After careful consideration, I've decided to look for a job with an organization where there is room for growth. Because I respect our relationship, I wanted to let you know about my job search and would like to know if you can provide a positive recommendation."*

HOW TO SAY IT

- Check with the Human Resources Department or your former direct manager to determine the organization's references policies. You may find that some are very strict and refuse to provide written recommendations. Some organizations may agree to provide only oral recommendations and then will supply only minimal information such as the date of hire, end date, job title, and salary history.

	Sample Scripts
Left on good terms	*"I worked for ABC Company two years ago and took time off to take care of my elderly mother. I'm ready to embark on a job search and am calling regarding the company's policy on references."*
Left on bad terms	*"Leanne, recently I was let go from ABC and I'm in the process of applying for a position as a marketing assistant with Modern Creative Solutions. References will be required and I'd like to discuss the possibility of coming to terms on the official reason for my termination."*

- Former managers can provide specifics on how your knowledge, skills, and abilities influenced the advancement of the department.

	Sample Scripts
Left on good terms	*"Bill, my wife has been transferred out of state and we'll be moving at the end of June. I'm planning on searching for a job in September and am compiling a list of references. I'd like to add your name since you have intimate knowledge of my strong work ethic."*

Left on bad terms	*"Jerry, after reflecting about my time with New Accounting I realize I made mistakes. I hope to grow professionally and bring my newfound knowledge to my next employer—which brings me to the point of this phone call. Potential employers will ask for references, and I'd like to discuss the way to best handle the situation."*

- Former colleagues and direct reports can serve as references because they worked with you on a daily basis and can provide details regarding your contribution to a team.

	Sample Scripts
Former colleague	*"Phil, I plan to begin a confidential job search; since we had great success with the Schuster project, I would like you to act as a reference. Specifically, I would like you to mention the role I took in gaining the Schuster account and how we worked as a team to meet the company's expectations. Is acting as one of my references something you are comfortable with?"*

Former direct report	*"Laurie, I'm applying for a management position in which I'll be overseeing fifty team members. Since we had a cooperative working relationship while I was with Smith and Associates, I would like you to serve as one of my references. May I use your name?"*

- Former associates or vendors can provide information on your professionalism and integrity when conducting business.

	Sample Scripts
Former vendor	*"When I was the operations manager for Star Time Electronics, I worked with you many times on coordinating the delivery of parts. You took note that I always made a point of getting the accounting department to provide you with prompt payment. I'm about to begin a job search, and since we had a good working relationship I'd like to know if you can serve as a reference."*
Former associate	*"I'm in the midst of a job search and am in need of a written recommendation for employment. Your name immediately came to mind.*

Over the years, we have shared referrals and contacts. Because of our collaborative relationship, I believe you can speak of my consultative selling skills."

- When asking references to speak on your behalf, listen to their responses carefully. Did they hesitate before agreeing? If you get the impression a reference is hedging, it's in your best interest to choose another individual to vouch for your qualifications. Or at the very least, acknowledge your reference's hesitation. Employers are good at reading between the lines and will pick up on any hesitation on the part of a reference.

	Sample Scripts
Reluctant reference	*"Sandy, I noticed you paused before agreeing to serve as my reference. If you have any reservations, I'd like to discuss them."* *"John, I approached you because you always made positive comments regarding my knowledge of insurance practices. I believe you would be an excellent reference and want to make sure this is a responsibility you are comfortable with."* *"Marie, it's understandable that you need time to think about my*

	request. I'll touch base with you early next week for your decision. How does that sound?"

- Once references have agreed to vouch for you, provide each with a point you want his or her message to focus on.

	Sample Scripts
Reference	*"Michael, thank you for agreeing to act as a reference. Since we collaborated on many projects together, no one can speak of my organizational skills better than you. I would like you to focus on my organizational skills when we worked on the ABC and XYZ projects."*
	"Carmen, since we've worked in the same department for over five years, it would be helpful if you emphasized my dedication and loyalty as a team member."

WHAT NOT TO SAY

- If you left a company on bad terms, don't be defensive when asking for a recommendation. For example, saying, *"Mike, I need a reference and if you say anything negative about me I will sue the company"* will only antagonize the situation. Instead, use the sample scripts on page 9 as a guide for how to approach an employer when you left in less-than-desirable circumstances.

- If a possible reference turns down your request, don't get upset and make disparaging comments. It's better to know in advance who is and is not comfortable speaking on your behalf.
- Approach references only when you have a clear understanding of the type of work you are looking for. Remember, you are asking individuals to vouch for you. They can do that successfully only if they have knowledge of your career goals and how their recommendations will help you.

HOW TO PREPARE REFERENCES

The moment you make the decision to look for a job, you should start looking for references. Once references have agreed to provide recommendations, prepare them for both oral and written recommendations.

Prepping References for Oral Recommendations

A phone call allows the interviewer to read the tone and enthusiasm in your reference's voice. In addition, interviewers like to speak to references so they can ask specific questions regarding your experience. When prepping references, follow these guidelines:

- Inform your references that they should answer only the questions they have intimate knowledge of. It's acceptable for references to say, *"I don't have enough insight to answer the question. Is there another question I can answer for you?"* when asked a question they are uncomfortable addressing.

- Some interviewers may call your references and say something like, *"Martha is applying for a position with our company. We would like to speak to individuals who know her very well. Can you recommend someone I can speak to?"* Interviewers use this tactic because they are aware the references you listed may have been prepped. For this reason, instead of asking your intended references questions, interviewers ask your references to recommend another person they can talk to. Let your references know that if they should encounter such a situation, they should graciously say, *"I'm available to answer questions regarding Martha's qualifications. Should you need to speak to another person, I'm sure Martha will be able to supply additional names. Are there any questions I can answer for you?"* Making such a statement will ensure that the interviewers are talking only to individuals you have screened.
- Once your references have agreed to provide recommendations, tell them what you would like them to home in on. Also let them know you plan to send them a list of key points, which will arrive via e-mail or postal mail. This way your references can keep the important points next to the phone for easy access.

Prepping References for Written Recommendations

Written recommendations are the norm in certain industries, such as education, health care, and the sciences, and part of the application process requires at least three letters of recommendation. That said, regardless of which industry you are in, you should always ask for letters of recommendation because you can submit the letters yourself at the end of an interview. Your references should follow these guidelines when writing your letters of recommendation:

- Give your references enough time to write a solid letter. At minimum, a week's notice should suffice, but a month's notice works best to ensure your references can accommodate your request.
- The reference letter should mention the length of time your reference has known you and the nature of your relationship (e.g., former supervisor, colleague, vendor, or business associate).
- Tell your references if the letter should be addressed to a specific person or if you plan to use it for more than one organization.
- Because prospective employers may want to follow up with a phone call to clarify issues or to probe further, ask your references if they are comfortable providing an oral recommendation should it be required.
- Once your references have agreed to help you, follow up by writing a letter or e-mail thanking each for his time and reiterating the key points discussed during your conversation, such as the deadline for the letter, your career objective, and information you'd like emphasized in the letter. (See page 18 for a sample follow-up letter.)

Power Words

affirm
assert
attest
corroborate
substantiate
recommend
testimonial
verify
validate

Power Phrases

confirm my background
endorse my candidacy
oral recommendation
positive letter of recommendation
provide a favorable reference
serve as a reference
vouch for my qualifications
write a reference letter

Sample Letters

Letter Requesting a Recommendation

Dear (Courtesy) (Last Name):

I'm preparing for a job search and was reviewing my past performance evaluations made when we both worked at Textile Imprints from 2001 to 2006. You took great care in mentioning how my analytical, problem-solving, and "get-it-done" approach contributed to the growth of the department.

With this in mind, I would like to know if you could write a letter of recommendation on my behalf. I'll follow up on this letter early next week to answer any questions you may have. In the meantime, you can reach me at 555-555-5555 if you want to speak to me before then.

Sincerely,

(signature)
Dominique Lebrock

Letter Thanking Your Reference

Dear (First Name or Last Name):

Thank you for agreeing to serve as a reference for me. As we discussed, I'm going to give my two-week notice to (Present Employer) and will be in need of references. I'll be applying for a sales position with companies such as Computer Associates, Symbol Technologies, and Veritas Software.

From my research, I've discovered the qualities that hiring organizations are seeking include a unique combination of team leadership, strategic planning, and business-development skills.

From firsthand knowledge, you are aware that those very characteristics allowed me to successfully average more than 80 percent sales growth within our territory, helping our company regain valuable market share.

This is the type of information interviewers are interested in knowing, and I'd appreciate it if you took special care to mention my skills in your letter of recommendation. For additional ideas, I have enclosed an updated version of my résumé, which provides a good summary of my accomplishments.

(Name), thanks again for taking the time out of your busy schedule to write a letter on my behalf. Should you have additional questions, I can be reached at 555-555-5555.

Sincerely,

(signature)

Barbara Manson

2

Preparing Your Thirty-Second Pitch

In thirty seconds you should be able to provide a snapshot of your background describing your professional qualifications and notable accomplishments. Having a compelling pitch will pique the interest of potential employers when they ask, *"Tell me about yourself"* during traditional interview settings (see Chapter 5 for information on different interview formats). You'll also need one when you're networking through informational interviews (see Chapter 4 for information on informational interviews).

HOW TO SAY IT

Whether you are new to the job market, are considering changing careers, are unemployed, or are gainfully employed, you can easily create a pitch that grabs the attention of the listener by following these three steps (see page 23 for sample pitches):

1. *Provide a brief introduction.* Make mention of your key attributes that are important to the position you are seeking. For example, "*During my ten years of experience as a sales manager, I have mastered the ability to coach, train, and motivate sales teams into reaching corporate goals*" is a solid opening statement.
2. *Provide a career summary of your most recent work history.* Your career summary is the meat of your pitch. As a result, you should include accomplishments you want the listener to be aware of. For example, "*Most recently, at the Widget Corporation, I was challenged with turning around a stagnant territory that ranked last in sales in the Northeastern region. Using strategies that have worked in the past, I developed an aggressive sales campaign that focused on cultivating new accounts and nurturing the existing client base. The results were tremendous. Within six months my sales team and I were able to revitalize the territory and boost sales by 65 percent*" is a strong rundown of accomplishments.

   If you have little or no work experience, you can create a summary from internship experiences, part-time work, and/or anything you've learned in classes that would be relevant to the job.
3. *Ask a question or make a comment.* Cap off your pitch with a question that stimulates conversation or with a comment that demonstrates your confidence in your abilities.

	Traditional Interview Settings	Informational Interviews
Sample question	*"What strategies are currently*	*"Do you know of an*

	under way to increase sales and morale within your sales department?"	*organization that would benefit from my qualifications?"*
Sample comment	*"My sales experience seems to fit in perfectly with the requirements specified in the job description."*	*"I believe that my accomplishments would benefit an organization that has lagging sales."*

WHAT NOT TO SAY

- Don't try to impress the listener with complicated language. Use words that you are comfortable with and that roll easily off your tongue.
- Don't try to wing it. Practice your introduction in front of family and friends until it sounds natural, not memorized.
- Never allude to problems regarding your job search by saying, *"I've been on lots of interviews but haven't received any job offers."* Sounding desperate will give the listener the impression that you are unemployable.
- Avoid rambling and keep your pitch brief. Specific details about your experiences and goals should be elaborated on once the questions and answers begin to flow.

Power Words

acquired
administered
advised
carried out
consulted
defined
delivered
drove
excelled
expanded
expedited
formulated
launched
maximized
persuaded
qualified
reached
restored
reviewed
stimulated
strengthened

Personal Characteristics

creative
determined
diligent
disciplined
independent
optimistic
personable
pleasant
positive
practical
proactive
productive
quick learner
receptive
reliable
resilient
resourceful
self-confident
sharp
successful
tenacious

Power Phrases

achieve win-win solutions
award-winning executive
chronicled success
consistent record of achievement
contributed to the success
delivered consistent results
demonstrated success
improved productivity
offer a well-rounded background
outstanding record of achievement
resolved discrepancies

routinely met quota
significant record of achievement
solid background
solution-oriented
strong ability to produce results

Sample Pitches

Informational Interviews

- *"As a property manager, I assist leasing consultants with filling vacancies. In addition, I maintain solid tenant relations by resolving critical issues in a timely fashion. I'm in search of a three-hundred-unit corporative in the New York area that is in need of someone who has experience in leasing, sales, and customer service. Do any facilities come to mind?"*
- *"My recent experience includes internships within a healthcare facility and behavioral medicine center as well as volunteer work with Mental Health for All. Through this experience, I have gained knowledge and skills in working with a cross-population of mental health patients. In addition, I have created effective discharge plans and referred individuals to appropriate community resources. Are you aware of any mental health facilities that have open position for a healthcare professional?"*
- *"The childhood development stage between five and twelve is, to me, the most critical in terms of academic and behavioral growth. For this reason, I strive to motivate students and generate interest in their education through incorporating textbook knowledge and real-life experiences into my lesson plans. I am confident I have*

the skills and positive attitude necessary to make a contribution to a school district in the Boston area."

- *"My management experience with New Star has strengthened my abilities in a number of areas, including team leadership, strategic planning, P&L management, and multistate operations expansion. Most notable, I was the key catalyst in a three-state expansion for New Star, writing a plan for implementing six new facilities that has reduced costs and improved customer service. I've enjoyed my experience with New Star and look forward to contributing to another organization in a management capacity."*
- *"As a food and beverage purchasing manager for the Delectable Culinary Institute, I solicit bids, prepare proposals, create purchase orders, and review requisitions from chefs. I achieved savings of fifteen thousand dollars within six months through my negotiation skills. I'm considering a career change to the sales industry. In view of my experience, do you believe I will be able to make a successful transition?"*
- *"While I was earning my bachelor degree in journalism, I interned at the local television station. My responsibilities were varied and included research, writing, and prepping guests for their television appearances. Currently, I am seeking an entry-level position in TV or print media. Are you aware of any openings?"*

Traditional Interviews

- *"As a paralegal, I have comprehensive experience in real estate law. My meticulous attention to detail allows me to prepare error-free legal memoranda, estoppels, and other legal documents. In addition, I participate in lease-review analysis and title and survey reviews to ensure smooth real estate closings. Are these the qualities you are looking for in a paralegal?"*

- *"As a network administrator, I'm an effective communicator who is able to explain complex processes in easy-to-understand terms for end users. Those qualities are complemented by my patient, methodical approach to problem resolution. In fact, I was successful in solving the majority of problem calls within my current employer's ten-minute requirement. Are these the types of qualities you seek in a network administrator?"*
- *"As a payroll specialist with ABC Company, I was charged with processing a biweekly payroll for over five thousand employees in all our offices in the United States. Ensuring compliance with all applicable state and federal wage and hour laws, I accurately verified time and attendance reports, resolved discrepancies regarding payroll, and reconciled the bank accounts. What are the main responsibilities for payroll specialists within your organization?"*
- *"With more then five years of experience in purchasing, supply, and logistics, I have a verifiable track record of exceeding quality, efficiency, and profit goals. Most recently, I was able to establish new vendor relationships securing a 35 percent cost reduction and a 60 percent inventory decrease. I'm confident that through my strong negotiation skills I can do the same for your company."*
- *"Since I've been a police officer for more than ten years you might wonder how my experience relates to a position as a fund-raising coordinator. The answer lies in my transferable skills and volunteer experience. Fund-raising relies heavily on relationship building, and as a police officer, I have experience interacting with community members and gaining their trust. This led to goodwill and a positive image for the police department. In addition, I*

served on the fund-raising committee for the local police association. My team and I achieved two of the highest fund-raising totals in the organization's history, reaching a total of two hundred thousand dollars. Considering my success, I am certain I can have a positive effect on the fund-raising efforts of your organization."

3

Making a Good Impression

Hiring decisions, for the most part, are made based on who the interviewer felt interviewed better—not on who is the most qualified for the position. Before the interview, the interviewer will have a mental picture of the perfect candidate's work ethic, character, and level of confidence. Based on the interviewer's expectations, an immediate judgment will be made on whether you would fit in with the company.

Based on this fact, your biggest role during the interview is to outperform your competition. Not only do you have to provide great responses to the questions posed but you have to take into account the way you approach the interview process, the way you dress, your nonverbal communication, and the way you handle anxiety. All of these factors sway an interviewer's perception of you and whether you will make a seamless transition into the open position.

INTERVIEW BASICS

Preparing the perfect answers to interview questions is important when getting ready for an interview. But far too often applicants forget that the following interview basics can make or break the interviewer's overall impression.

- ***Punctuality.*** Arrive ten to fifteen minutes before the interview is set to begin. The extra time will give you the opportunity to refresh your appearance in the restroom and to collect your thoughts before you enter the interview room. Don't arrive more than twenty minutes before the scheduled interview. The interviewer may be in a meeting or participating in another interview and will be distracted knowing that you are waiting. If you are running late, give the interviewer a call with an estimated time of arrival.
- ***Completing the application.*** An application is a legal document, but a résumé is not. This is why you are required to add your signature to the application indicating that all the information you provided is accurate. For this reason, it is important to complete the application in its entirety rather than writing "See résumé" in sections that require you to repeat information that already appears on your résumé.
- ***Résumé copies and supporting materials.*** You should always bring at least two copies of your résumé (printed on résumé paper) to the interview in a professional résumé folder. You should also come prepared with any supporting materials you think would help the interviewer gain thorough knowledge of your previous work and accomplishments.

Depending on the field you're interviewing in, supporting materials can include copies of college transcripts, degrees, certificates of completion, and academic awards; copies of positive performance evaluations, awards, and letters from customers praising your work; letters of recommendation; or writing samples. (See Chapter 1 for letters of recommendation guidelines.) If the interviewer doesn't ask for supporting materials you can offer to leave copies for her at the end of the interview.

- ***Interacting with others.*** Decision makers take into account their assistants' opinions of candidates when making hiring decisions. For this reason, treat everyone you encounter during the interview professionally and with respect.
- ***Handshake.*** Provide a firm handshake and greet the interviewer using her last name—use the interviewer's first name only if given permission to do so.

WHAT NOT TO DO

- Don't chew gum or have a mint in your mouth during an interview since doing so will distract the interviewer.
- Don't smoke before the interview since the cigarette or cigar smell will latch on to your clothing.
- Don't leave your cell phone on since you may receive a call in the middle of the interview. This includes not leaving your phone on vibrate since an incoming call will still be noticeable in a quiet room.

INTERVIEW DRESS CHECKLIST

Whether you are applying for a position in a corporate environment or in a relaxed, creative field, a polished, neat look is always required. To find out exactly how to dress for the interview, call and ask an HR representative for a recommendation or pass by the company to see what the employees entering and leaving the building are wearing. In this section, I list guidelines for selecting what to wear to an interview, regardless of the industry you're interviewing in.

Tips for Everyone

- Wear clothes that are comfortable, clean, and well pressed. Your shoes should be shined and be appropriate for the outfit you are wearing.
- If wearing a suit, choose black, navy blue, or gray and pair it with a simple white or cream-colored dress shirt.
- Make sure your hair and nails are well groomed.
- Use breath spray and visually check to make sure food isn't stuck between your teeth.
- Since you don't know if the interviewer is allergic or will find the smell offensive, don't wear cologne or perfume.
- Cover tattoos and remove body piercings.
- Don't carry a backpack. Instead, carry a briefcase or bring along a portfolio.
- Don't wear a wrinkled or ill-fitting suit.

Tips for Women

- If applying for a position in a less than traditional environment, you can choose to wear a blazer and skirt or slacks—skirts should be at or below the knee. Always wear hosiery with skirts.

- To add color and style to your outfit, wear a simple scarf or single piece of jewelry; if you wear earrings, choose a conservative pair.
- Leave the bulky purse at home. Use a tiny bag or a briefcase.
- Wear nail polish in a light, neutral color; use a light touch on makeup.
- Steer clear of clothes that are trendy, too tight, or revealing.
- Stay away from wearing spike heels and open-toed or backless shoes.

Tips for Men

- If applying for a position in a less than traditional environment, you can choose to wear a dark blazer or sport coat with dress pants. Or you can wear a pair of dress pants with a long-sleeved dress shirt and tie, no jacket.
- If wearing a tie, keep it conservative with colors to match your suit or jacket.
- Choose a belt that matches your shoes.
- Wear minimal jewelry; a dress watch is fine.
- Beards and mustaches should be neatly trimmed.
- Don't wear white sports socks. Instead, wear dress socks to match your suit.
- Don't wear earrings.

NONVERBAL COMMUNICATION

It is widely reported that 55 percent of communication is nonverbal. That's why you should be aware of your tone of voice, body language, posture, and facial expressions during an interview. Here are some basic guidelines for improving your nonverbal communication skills:

- Maintain eye contact throughout the interview because it is a sign that you are confident in your ability to do the job. Though it's important to maintain eye contact, avoid locking eyes with the interviewer for the entire conversation since that will make for an uncomfortable situation. It's important to strike a balance between maintaining eye contact and casually looking down at your notebook.
- To appear friendly and put the interviewer at ease, smile throughout the interview.
- Lean forward or tilt your head to one side to demonstrate interest in what the interviewer is saying.
- Be aware of your nervous habits, such as twirling your hair or touching your nose, chin, ear, arm, or clothing since the interviewer may interpret that as a lack of confidence.
- When being escorted to the interview room or when being given a tour of the facility, walk with your head held high and shoulders straight to demonstrate confidence.

WHAT NOT TO DO

- Don't squint your eyes since that demonstrates you may be dissatisfied with what the interviewer is saying.
- Don't twitch, move from side to side, or shift your weight while sitting since the interviewer will take

that as a sign of insecurity. Instead, sit erect with your legs crossed or leaning to the side.

- Make sure you don't cross your arms when the interviewer is asking a question since that can be construed as a defensive sign.

OVERCOMING ANXIETY

With so much on the line during an interview, it's only natural to find it challenging to rely on a set of skills (interviewing) that you've used only a few times in your life. It's perfectly common to have interview jitters, knowing that so much is at stake. Interviewers understand this and expect candidates to be a little nervous but, at the same time, anticipate that the nervousness won't be a distraction. To ease your anxiety and leave a positive impression on the interviewer, keep the following in mind:

- Though the ultimate purpose of an interview is to receive a job offer, don't put too much weight on landing an offer instantly. It's important to note that the immediate objective is for you to learn about the organization and for the interviewer to learn more about you. Going into an interview with this mindset will allow you to put the interview process in perspective.
- Prepare solid answers to questions you are afraid to be asked. For example, if you have a job-hopper image or an unemployment gap and believe the interviewer will probe into this issue, forming a response before the interview will ease your nerves. (See

Chapter 11 for how to discuss previous career challenges.)

- Though it's impossible to determine the exact questions you will be asked, practice answering potential questions out loud in front of a friend or family member to get all the kinks out of your answers. Even if you aren't asked the exact questions you prepared for, going through the process of saying your answers out loud will work wonders when it comes time to articulate a response to similar questions. (See Part III for tips on how to answer interview questions.)
- Keep in mind that the reason you were invited in for an interview out of a stack of other applications is because the interviewer is interested in you, so you are already at an advantage.
- While in the waiting room, reflect on your past accomplishments, performance appraisals, and/or any awards you have received. Reminding yourself of your qualifications will give you confidence.

PART II

Adapting to Different Interview Formats and Interviewer Styles

4

Informational Interviews—The Fast Track to a New Job

The purpose of an informational interview is to learn about the culture of a company and/or industry and to gain advice on hiring and interviewing practices of organizations that pique your interest. For a job interview, you are invited to interview for an open position, but an informational interview differs in two ways:

- It is up to you to set the agenda and prepare questions in advance to keep the conversation flowing. (See pages 45–48 for sample informational interview questions.)
- The focus of the interview is more on your contact's knowledge and guidance, and less on your qualifications. You are there to gather information.

HOW TO SAY IT

Setting Up Informational Interviews

- Develop a well-rounded network by jotting down the names of your personal, professional, and Internet contact base. Use the list as a springboard for setting up informational interviews.

    - Personal contacts include relatives, acquaintances, friends, family doctor, lawyer, and neighbors.
    - Professional contacts include colleagues, business associates, vendors, and direct reports.
    - Internet contacts include online networking and Internet job clubs you participate in.

- Choose whether you want to get in touch with your contacts by phone or in writing. Once you decide how you want to make contact, you should keep the following elements in mind:

    - *Letter.* The first paragraph should explain the reason you are writing and the name of the person who referred you or how you found the person's contact information (e.g., newspaper article or alumni association). The body of the letter is made up of one to two paragraphs maximum. Tell the reader about yourself and your goals and aspirations. Include information on how you believe he can be of assistance. In the closing paragraph, thank your contact and include plans to follow up by phone to set up an informational interview. (See pages 42–44 for sample informational interview letters.)
    - *Phone call.* The introductory call should include the reason for the call, how you received the person's

name (if she is not an acquaintance), information regarding your background, and a solicitation for a meeting. (See pages 41–42 for sample informational interview telephone scripts.)

During the Informational Interview

- Respect your contacts and listen to the advice they offer. If you constantly reply with, *"Yeah, but . . ."* or *"I already tried that and it didn't work,"* you will slowly jeopardize the relationship.
- Because most people will be gracious, they will leave it up to you to end the interview. For this reason, no matter how well you believe the conversation is going, don't go beyond the time frame you provided when you set up the meeting. To gracefully end the meeting state, *"Mr. Bloomberg, our time is almost over, and before we end this meeting, I'd like to ask one more question. . . ."*
- At the end of the interview, ask your contact for names of three individuals who she can introduce you to.

After the Informational Interview

- Use the Informational Interview/Networking Evaluation Form on page 50 to evaluate what you learned and the advice you will follow through on.
- From time to time, update your contacts regarding your progress. Doing so will leave the door open for further communication should you need their assistance again. (See page 44 for a sample progress letter.)
- Send a note thanking each contact for the information provided during the interview. The letter can be short and sweet and doesn't have to go into great detail. (See page 44 for a sample thank-you letter.)

Power Words

apply
appreciate
coordinate
determine
discover
examine
explore
inquire
investigate
learn
meet
potential
request
research
set up

Personal Characteristics

capable
committed
competent
cooperative
dedicated
dependable
focused
optimistic
talented

Power Phrases

any insights would be greatly appreciated
arrange a meeting
ask you some questions
conducting industry research
considering changing careers
desire to move forward
determine the best approach
explore opportunities
gather firsthand information
looking for career advancement
meet to discuss
offer advice
provide specific details
seeking a position
seeking an opportunity
twenty-minute conversation
value your advice
welcome new opportunities

Sample Telephone Scripts

Friend/Family/Acquaintance

- *"Dan, thank you for your condolences and for attending my mom's funeral. As you know, I took four years off to care for her and now that she has passed I'm looking to reenter the workforce. I'm sure the job market has changed significantly over the years and since you embarked on a job search recently, I would like to know if we can set up a time to chat so you can fill me in on the latest job-search trends."*
- *"Nicole, I've made the decision to make a transition from marketing to sales and would like to know more about the type of interview questions I can expect to receive. Since you have been in sales for over five years, I'd like to sit down with you and pick your brain. I'm not looking for a job but rather advice on how to make a successful transition. Could we meet at your convenience so I can ask a few questions?"*

Cold Call

- *"Thank you for taking my phone call. My name is Philip Martinez, and I was referred by Tracy Frey. I recently found myself in a job search and I would like to meet with you to discuss opportunities in the telecommunications industry. Can you set aside twenty minutes this week to meet with me?"*
- *"Marissa Montana, a colleague of yours, gave me your contact information. My name is Joe Cumeisky and I am pursuing a career change and she thought you might be able to offer advice about the dos and don'ts of launching a human resource career. Would you have a few minutes to meet with me early next week?"*

- *"My name is Justin Rodriquez and I'm a student at NYU and I'm considering a career in journalism. I'm conducting research and would like to speak to professionals in the communications industry. Would you be willing to meet with me to talk about the field?"*

Follow-Up Call

- *"My name is Kelly Monroe, and I sent you a letter of introduction last week along with my résumé requesting an informational interview. As promised, I'm following up to arrange a meeting."*
- *"Mr. Jefferson, this is Mark Heaton. I'm following up on an e-mail I sent regarding my job search. To refresh your memory, I'm a purchasing agent who is seeking information on how to best prepare for an interview. I'd welcome your thoughts and ideas on how I can get in front of decision makers."*

Sample Letters

Letter of Introduction

Dear Mr. Lauer:

I found your name in the Hofstra Law alumni book. After reading your biography and learning about the strides you have taken in the field, I am seeking your guidance.

Like you, I am Hispanic and was impressed by the fact that you own one of the most respected criminal defense law firms in Suffolk County. As a prelaw student, I have narrowed my career interests to either criminal or environmental law. Since I am undecided between the two, I am seeking advice on the pros and cons of each.

Considering your background as a former district attorney and the success of your criminal defense firm, I believe you can offer the insight I'm in search of.

I will contact your office the week of June 15 to set up an informational interview. Please let your assistant know you are expecting my call so she will be prepared to put my call through. In the meantime, I can be reached at 631-555-5555.
Sincerely,

(signature)
Brenda Martinez

Personal Referral Letter

Dear Mr. Hemingway:
I recently had an informative conversation with John Meyers from Medical Solutions in San Diego. Mr. Meyers recommended I contact you to gain information about pharmaceutical sales.

As you are aware, the pharmaceutical industry is very competitive. I would appreciate any advice you can offer on how I can open doors. Specifically, I would like to know how to conduct an effective job search and what decision makers are looking for in an ideal candidate.

I will call you Tuesday morning at 10 a.m. to discuss the possibility of getting together for a quick meeting.
Sincerely,

(signature)
Duane White

Thank-You Letter

Dear Tom:

Thank you for taking time out of your busy schedule to meet with me. You provided great insight and clarified many issues. Based on our conversation, I feel I am on the right track.

I have already begun implementing the strategies you suggested. I'll keep you updated on my progress.

Sincerely,

(signature)
Shane Sepersaude

Progress Letter

Dear Mr. Cohen:

Thank you for spending time with me Tuesday morning to discuss my job search. From our conversation, I gained practical tips that I started implementing right away. I focused on your ideas for making my résumé more powerful. Taking your advice, I submitted my résumé to a recruiter, and I have an interview scheduled for next week.

I truly appreciated the opportunity to meet you and learn the ins and outs of the engineering field. Thanks to you, I'm now on the right path. I'll keep you updated on my search.

Sincerely,

(signature)
Kai Sher

INFORMATIONAL INTERVIEW QUESTIONS

Make the best of the informational interviews by developing questions before your meeting. Determining which questions to ask depends on your situation. Take inventory of the areas you need the most help in and create questions surrounding those issues. Keep in mind that you don't have to stick to one line of questioning. It's best to add a mixture of questions to make the most of the informational interview.

Questions Regarding the Interview and Hiring Process

- **What types of questions should I expect when interviewing for a job in this field?** Knowing the types of questions to expect at a job interview will provide you with a competitive advantage. Pay close attention to the information your contact provides and use it as part of your interview preparation. (See Chapters 8 to 12 for sample interview question and answers.)
- **The job market is very tight. How can I stand apart from other candidates vying for the same position?** Does your contact suggest making changes to your résumé? Does she suggest using a specific approach in your cover letter? Listen carefully to your contact's suggestions for standing apart from other candidates because he or she has probably been in the industry for several years and knows what it takes to really impress an employer in your field.
- **Given my skills and background is it realistic to expect that hiring managers will be interested in**

me? A good contact will be honest with you and reveal your strengths and weaknesses as he sees them. With the information provided, you will have a firm grasp of your most marketable traits and those you need to improve on to become more desirable to a hiring organization.

- **I want to be sure that my résumé will open doors to interviews. Would you mind reviewing my résumé and providing feedback?** The moment your résumé lands on a hiring manager's desk, a judgment is made on your qualifications and work ethic. For this reason, don't underestimate the integral part a résumé plays in the interview process. Your contact may provide insight on how to effectively market yourself on paper.
- **What salary range can a person with my skills and background demand in the job market?** Knowing the salary you can expect will help you prepare for the salary negotiations process before the first interview. (See Chapter 15 for additional information on effective salary negotiation strategies.)

Questions Regarding Industry Hiring Practices

- **How do hiring organizations recruit top talent?** Are hiring managers in your industry using the Internet, classified ads, and/or recruiters to find talent? The answer to this question can have a direct impact on how you search for a job.
- **Do you have written job descriptions of positions in this field/company that you can share with me?** Job descriptions can provide an insider's view on the skills that are important to hiring organizations.

For example, if you are in quality assurance and most job descriptions you come across stress the importance of complying with safety standards, it's a good bet that hiring managers will broach the subject during the interview. The information you glean from job descriptions can be used to prepare for an interview. (See Chapter 7 for more information on how to effectively use job descriptions.)

- **In this industry, are promotions based on seniority or accomplishments?** Some companies still hold on to the old-school mentality in which old-timers, no matter their accomplishments or lack thereof, are offered an opportunity to move up the ladder before a new hire. If opportunity for growth is important to you, then you deserve to know that if you put 100 percent in to your work you will be rewarded accordingly.

Questions Regarding Your Peers

- **What is the educational background of the most successful people in the industry?** It's important to know if you need to acquire additional education or training to compete against your peers. If the interviewer states that a certain education level is needed and you don't possess it, you can ask the following question: *"I currently have an associate's degree and I'm unable to return to earn a bachelor degree. Will the lack of a four-year degree hinder my chances of landing a position?"*
- **What are the characteristics of the people in this industry?** Those in the same industry usually share common characteristics. For example, accounting professionals are known to be analytical, whereas

marketing professionals are recognized for their creativity. Knowing the qualities that are most sought after in your field will allow you to compare the similarities between you and your peers. You will also know which characteristics you should stress about yourself during an interview.

Bringing the Informational Interview to a Close

- **Thank you for taking the time to offer me advice. Before we bring this meeting to a close, is there something else I should know regarding hiring or job search practices that we didn't cover?** Once you have access to a well-informed contact you don't want to leave any stone unturned. Asking if he has additional information may jog your contact's memory and he may offer suggestions that will be useful to you.
- **Can you provide me with the names of individuals I might contact for more information?** If you left a good impression your contact will provide names of others who may have tips, strategies, and leads you will benefit from. When provided with additional names, be sure to follow up. You shouldn't pass up opportunities that can prove to be fruitful.
- **Would you be willing to answer more questions, by phone or in person, if I need additional advice?** You never know how your search will progress and if you'll need additional assistance down the road. For this reason, it's important to leave the door open for further communication.

Networking List

Name	Phone Number	Physical Address	E-mail Address	Relation	Phone Call or Letter?
1.					
2.					
3.					
4.					
5.					
6.					
7.					
8.					
9.					
10.					
11.					
12.					
13.					
14.					
15.					
16.					
17.					
18.					
19.					
20.					

Informational Interview/Networking Evaluation Form

Name of Contact ______________ **Company** __________

Address ______________________________________

Office Phone ________________ **E-mail** _____________

Information regarding the interviewer that I learned

____

____

____

What did I learn from the conversation?

____

____

____

From what I learned, what am I going to put into action right away?

____

____

____

Name and contact information of three referrals

1. ____
2. ____
3. ____

Companies interviewer suggested I research

1. ____
2. ____
3. ____

5

Effectively Manage Different Interview Formats

Interview settings have become more sophisticated over the years as employers find it increasingly difficult to choose the right candidate. In the hopes of getting a clearer picture of applicants and lower the risk of a bad hire, you may be asked to participate in a series of different interview formats.

Though the thought of going on interview after interview for the same company may sound intimidating, the more time you spend with the company, the more you learn about the position, the organization, and its people. You can use the information gathered to determine if the organization suits your goals and objectives.

An invitation to participate in a round of interviews is also a sign that an employer is interested in your candidacy. The more interviews you go on for the same company, the closer you are to a job offer.

Quick Tip

From your perspective, the interview is an opportunity to sell your qualifications and evaluate the position. For those reasons, you should ask questions of the interviewers, regardless of the interview format. See Chapter 13 for sample questions you can ask.

TYPE OF INTERVIEW FORMATS TO EXPECT

Common interview formats are screening, one-on-one, stress, panel, peer, and group. Each format has its own characteristics, advantages, and disadvantages. If you have past interviewing experience, you can use that to determine which interview format is standard in your industry.

You can also anticipate the type of interview settings you may encounter by asking contacts during informational interviews. That said, all the interview formats discussed in this chapter can be used in any industry or profession no matter the size of the hiring organization. For this reason, you should become familiar with each and be prepared to expect any one of them.

GETTING PAST THE SCREENING INTERVIEW

Usually conducted by a human resources representative, screening interviews are used by hiring organizations as a way to weed out unqualified, overqualified, or overpriced candidates. During a screening interview, you will be asked questions that clarify or confirm information you provided on your résumé. Screening interviews can be held by phone or in person.

Interview Characteristics

- During the course of the interview, you will be asked a set of predetermined questions that focus on your experience, skills, and education.
- The screening interview is not designed to determine the most qualified candidate but rather is used as a vehicle to establish a short list of applicants who meet the minimum requirements.
- The interview may consist of only a few questions and may last an average of thirty minutes.
- If the screening interview is conducted in person and you pass the minimum requirements, you may be asked to participate in a one-on-one interview with the hiring manager immediately.
- If the screening interview is conducted over the phone and you pass the minimum requirements, you may be asked to set up an in-person interview during the call.
- Computer screening interviews can be as simple as completing an application online or more comprehensive, such as a personality test and/or a set of intense interview questions. For example, you may be asked open-ended questions such as, *"Why should we hire you?"* or *"What is your greatest weakness?"*

Advantages

- If you don't meet the minimum requirements, your time isn't wasted on going through an in-person interview.

- You will have the opportunity to learn more about the open position and be better prepared when you meet with the decision maker.
- If the screening interview is conducted by phone or computer, you will be able to have your résumé and cheat sheet with relevant facts and accomplishments by your side.

Disadvantages

Phone or In-Person Screening Interview

- The screener is not a decision maker and is solely responsible for confirming that you meet the minimum requirements. Only then will you be invited to talk with the decision maker.
- The screener may not be familiar with all the job functions and may get lost if you use a lot of technical jargon or buzzwords familiar only to those in the industry. For this reason, your responses should be given in plain English.
- If the interview is over the phone, you may get caught at an inopportune time and not be prepared to participate in the screening process when the interviewer calls.
- Phone interviews don't provide the benefit of an in-person interview, which is more intimate and allows you and the screener to read each other's nonverbal communication.

Computer Screening Interview

- The system may have a timer and will register how long it takes you to answer interview questions. If you are a slow typist, this may work against you since the interviewer may assume that you took long to respond because you aren't providing truthful answers or that you are unqualified to answer the questions posed.

- You may not understand a question and don't have the opportunity to ask for clarification.
- You won't be able to elaborate on sticking points when presented with multiple choice answers. For example, if asked for salary requirements you may have to check off an amount without indicating that it is negotiable.

HOW TO SAY IT

Phone and In-Person Screening Interviews

- During a phone interview, the interviewer cannot see your facial expressions. For this reason you should communicate your enthusiasm for the position by your tone of voice.
- Have your résumé, cheat sheet, and pencil and paper next to the phone at all times.
- Inform all members of your household that you are in the midst of a job search and that they should answer the phone professionally. If you have young children, tell them not to answer the phone.
- When in a job search, always expect that it's a potential employer when the phone rings. If you are not able to talk don't pick up the phone. Let the call go to voice mail and return the call when you are able to do so without distractions.
- Send a thank-you note. (See Chapter 14 for information on sending thank-you letters.)
- Though the screener has little or no influence on the hiring decision, she does have the authority to invite

you to participate in the next round of interviews. With this in mind, take the screening interview seriously and always answer the questions fully.
- Treat the screener with respect; show up on time and dress professionally.

Computer screening interviews
- Check your responses for spelling and grammatical errors before you hit the submit button.
- Write out responses to typical interview questions—such as *"Tell me about yourself," "Where do you want to be in five years?" "What is your greatest strength and weakness?"*—ahead of time so you can copy and paste the responses into the computer form.

ONE-ON-ONE INTERVIEW

The one-on-one interview is a face-to-face meeting between a decision maker and you. This type of interview is usually conducted at the company headquarters and lasts between thirty and sixty minutes. It is straightforward and the interviewer doesn't rely on any tactics except conversation to discuss the job requirements and your qualifications.

Interview Characteristics

- The interview may be preceded by small talk or chitchat. For example, the interviewer may ask, *"How's the weather?"* or *"Did you find us okay?"* to break the ice.
- The interviewer will ask direct questions about your background, education, skills, experience, personality, ethics, and leadership skills.

- The interviewer will usually use your résumé as a guideline for questioning.

Advantages

- A one-on-one setting allows you to easily home in on the interviewer's nonverbal communication. You can assess his body language and demeanor to determine if your responses are on target.
- Both you and the interviewer can be more relaxed because there are no outside influences.
- Building rapport in a one-on-one situation is easier since you have to adapt your communication style to the needs of only one interviewer.
- If you have gone on interviews before, you have most likely participated in a one-on-one setting and can easily draw from your experiences to determine what to expect.
- You will be speaking to a decision maker.

Disadvantages

- The interview may seem casual and you can easily let your guard down and reveal information you ordinarily wouldn't.
- The decision to hire you or ask you back for a second interview is based on only one person's opinion.

HOW TO SAY IT

- Your responses should be truthful. Avoid providing answers based solely on what you believe the interviewer wants to hear.
- If you are having difficulty thinking of an answer, repeat the question as part of your response. For

example if asked, *"Where do you see yourself in five years?"* you can begin your response with, *"In five years I see myself . . ."* Using this method will buy you time when responding to questions that require more thought or when a response is not at the tip of your tongue.

- It's acceptable to pause for a few seconds and digest the question before jumping in with an answer.
- Remain positive throughout the interview and do not reveal negative information regarding your current/previous work situation. Doing so will open areas of questioning that may hurt your chances of landing a job offer.
- Send a thank-you note.

WHAT NOT TO SAY

- Don't act like a politician and provide answers that will serve your agenda. Answer the question the interviewer is asking.
- Don't go off on tangents and provide irrelevant information. Discuss only facts pertinent to the position and that match your experience with the needs of the organization.
- Don't be too brief since the interviewer may assume you either lack experience, don't know enough about the position, or are trying to hide something.
- Don't provide long responses since you may lose the interviewer's interest.

EASE THROUGH THE STRESS INTERVIEW

Some interviewers may choose to conduct a stress interview for positions that are very demanding. Stress interviews often take place because the interviewer wants to simulate a real-life stressful situation by creating an uncomfortable interview environment to observe how you react. Based on your reactions, the interviewer will presume he has a good indication of how you handle on-the-job stress. Stress interviews are not limited to a specific industry and can run the gamut from customer service to teaching to social work to sales.

Interview Characteristics

- The interviewer may remain quiet when you enter the room waiting to see if you take the initiative to introduce yourself.
- The interviewer may be on the phone or reading documents when you enter the room and not acknowledge you.
- Without making an introduction, the interviewer may begin asking tough interview questions the moment you walk into the room.
- Once you have finished answering a question, the interviewer may remain silent implying that you should keep talking to make you think your response wasn't adequate.
- The interviewer may home in on a certain aspect of your background such as your education and experience and begin to attack it.
- The interviewer may use rapid-fire questioning, not allowing you to answer any of them fully.

- You may be asked to undertake a project with unclear or nonexistent instructions.

Advantage

- When a company conducts a stress interview it indicates that the open position may be demanding. You can use that tip to determine whether you want to participate in additional rounds of interviews or whether you would accept a job offer should it be extended.

Disadvantages

- You may feel too stressed to provide coherent answers that demonstrate your ability to do the job.
- You may like everything the company has to offer, but get turned off by the interviewing style and decide not to participate in another round of interviews.
- You may find it difficult to be yourself and may rush your responses.

HOW TO SAY IT

- If the interviewer ignores you when you walk in the room, introduce yourself and begin talking about your experience and qualifications. For example, you can extend your hand and say, *"Ms. Irwin, thank you for taking the time to meet with me today. I trust you had the opportunity to read my résumé. I would like to draw your attention to . . ."*
- If the interviewer remains silent after you respond to a question, you can choose to reiterate your response or you can move the conversation along by providing additional information regarding your qualifications or asking a question relevant to the job description.

Quick Tip

There may be times when you are dealing with an interviewer who is either inexperienced or has a negative attitude. In those cases, you may feel as though you are in a stress interview even though you're not. You have to rely on your gut instinct to make the proper determination.

- When asked a question, take the time to collect your thoughts and feel free to ask for clarification if you need to.
- If the stress interview takes place in a conference room where a flip chart or dry-erase board is available use them as props to alleviate your stress. For example, you can draw diagrams or pie charts to illustrate your point.
- If you feel comfortable doing so, it's acceptable to inform the interviewer that you are aware a stress interview is taking place and you are willing to work a few hours so he can see firsthand how well you perform under stressful situations.
- Send a thank-you note.

WHAT NOT TO SAY

- Since the stress interview is a test to see how you react under pressure, the interviewer will place more emphasis on your demeanor than on your responses. For this reason, avoid getting angry or making defensive statements such as, *"I don't like the way you are conducting this interview."*

JUGGLING THE PANEL INTERVIEW

The panel interview is a meeting with more than one interviewer at the same time. They are often used to cut back on the time it takes to recruit candidates and to allow more than one person to have a say in who is hired. The interviewers can consist of a human resources representative, manager, and a peer. Usually one person acts as the panel leader.

Interview Characteristics

- The panel interview can share some or all of the same characteristics of a stress interview.
- The interview may take place in a conference room setting, not in a cozy office. The panelists will sit on one side of the table and you will sit across from them.
- There will be a panel leader who will lead the discussion and keep the interview moving along. You will be able to determine the leader because she will most likely introduce each panel member to you.
- Panel members may be assigned questions relevant to their roles in the organization. For example, the human resources representative will be interested in cultural fit, the hiring manager in the technical skills needed to perform the job, and a peer on whether or not you can work in a team environment.
- Possible formats:
    - Two or more interviewers may play off each other. They may have different roles (bad cop, good cop).
    - Only one interviewer may ask the questions while the rest of the interviewer(s) observe and take notes.

  - Each interviewer may ask a question or series of questions based on one specific topic.

- The interviewers may allow follow-up questions and dialogue or they may simply move to the next question with no comment.

Advantages

- Since many positions require candidates to interact closely with different departments, the panel interview allows you to meet potential colleagues. This is a great way to determine if you click with current employees before you accept a position, if one is extended.
- The hiring decision isn't based solely on the impression of one person, and if you made a poor impression on one interviewer, another may have felt a connection and will go to bat for you.
- You have the opportunity to witness the dynamics of the team and get a better picture of the organization and its employees.
- Because time is a valuable resource, a panel interview allows the interview process to go quickly since you will meet all key people in one meeting.

Disadvantages

- Establishing rapport may be difficult because you have to adapt your communication style to several people.
- If the panel isn't trained properly, one member can easily dominate the interview process with his own agenda.

HOW TO SAY IT

- If you know you will be having a panel interview when setting up the meeting, ask for an organizational chart and a list of who will be attending the interview. This will help you know the key players within the organization.
- If the leader of the panel doesn't introduce the rest of the interviewers, ask her to make the introduction.
- To build rapport, use the interviewer's names frequently as you answer interview questions. Use only last names unless given permission to do otherwise.
- When answering a question, respond to the interviewer who asked it while scanning the rest of the interviewers across the table. Finish your response by returning your focus to the interviewer who asked the question.
- When asking a follow-up question, direct the question to the interviewer who asked the original question.
- Send a separate thank-you note to each interviewer.

PEER INTERVIEW

Peer interviews are usually conducted after the hiring manager has interviewed a candidate and made the determination that the candidate meets the requirements for the position. The peer interview team is usually composed of company loyalists—individuals who are enthusiasts and consistently contribute to the growth of the organization. They represent a cross-section of the organization's makeup (i.e., a blend of employees from different races, age groups, and levels of work experience). These employees are given the opportunity to interview candidates and provide feedback before the hiring decision is made. Although their opinions are valued, it is usually up to management to make a final hiring decision.

Interview Characteristics

- The interview may be conducted in a one-on-one or panel interview setting.
- Some organizations will properly prepare each employee by setting a clear agenda and structured questions. Others simply conduct peer interviews without proper training, making the interview setting feel less formal than other formats.
- To avoid gut-reaction judgments, peer interviewers are usually required to complete a form that scores candidates on work-related skills, knowledge, and abilities.
- The questioning may be more laid-back in an effort to encourage you to let your guard down.

Advantages

- Employees don't always know what happens down in the "trenches," so this is your opportunity to discover facts managers may not be privvy to.
- Peer interviews are helpful because they allow you and your potential colleagues an opportunity to meet before an offer is extended. Through this format, you will be able to determine if your potential new coworkers are people who you respect and look forward to partnering with.
- Studies indicate that organizations who participate in peer interviewing have a lower turnover rate and enjoy a more harmonious working enviroment than those organizations that do not.

- You will have a better understanding of the corporate culture and be able to make an educated decision about whether you want to work there.

Disadvantages

- The atmosphere might feel casual, giving you a false sense of security. Thus you may let down your guard and divulge sensitive information you may not have otherwise revealed.
- Your peers may base their decisions on personality factors instead of your ability to perform the required tasks.
- Your peers may be inexperienced interviewers, so it may be up to you to limit the number of awkward moments and make them feel comfortable.

HOW TO SAY IT

- Treat each peer with respect because she has some degree of influence on whether you are extended a job offer.
- Send a thank-you note.

WHAT NOT TO SAY

- Do not be overly friendly and do not use slang when responding to questions—even if the interviewer does. Remain professional at all times.

GROUP INTERVIEW

A group interview consists of more than one candidate being interviewed simultaneously for the same position.

The purpose of a group interview is to observe each candidate's leadership, communication, interpersonal, and team-work skills in an interactive setting. Group interviews are often used when the work situation involves a lot of team interaction or for a large corporation that hires large numbers of staff.

Interview Characteristics

- As in the panel interview, a group interview may have more than one interviewer in attendance.
- The opening questions tend to be more general and simple in nature, and the more difficult ones come later when group members are more relaxed.
- Possible formats:
    - The interviewers may split the group into teams and provide a hypothetical problem or task. They then observe how all the candidates interact with each other and how the answers are presented. The interviewers are not involved in the group discussion and are present just to observe and scrutinize behavior.
    - The interviewers may ask a question to a specific candidate or they may throw out a question and see who responds and who stays in the background.
- Immediately after the group interview, one-on-one interviews may be conducted for those who performed well during the group interview.

Advantages

- Knowing all the answers isn't necessary since you are working as a team to complete a project. This strength in numbers allows you to easily showcase your strengths while others in the group will make up for your shortcomings.

- You will have the opportunity to meet your direct competition.

Disadvantages

- In a group setting you may become an exaggerated version of yourself. If you are aggressive by nature, you may become more aggressive. And if you are shy you may become shyer.
- The temptation to compare yourself to the candidates during the interview may distract you from the focus of the interview.
- Stage fright might set in, and you can be overshadowed by the performance of another candidate.

HOW TO SAY IT

- Share your ideas, answer questions, and make the rest of the candidates feel comfortable to share their own by listening to them and acknowledging their thoughts.
- Answer questions while allowing the rest of the candidates to speak.
- Be aware of the interviewers' presence but avoid focusing on them.
- Provide positive feedback and encouragement to your teammates.
- Send a separate thank-you note to each of the interviewers.

WHAT NOT TO SAY

- Don't participate in a power struggle with another candidate over an idea or leadership role and make statements such as, *"I was talking. Please don't interrupt."*
- Interact with the whole group and avoid one-on-one side conversations.

6

Recognizing and Adapting to Different Interviewer Styles

Interviewers tend to make a snap judgment on your suitability for the job based on whether there is a connection between the two of you. This means that if you fit the job description to a tee but fail to build trust and credibility during the interview, you may be overlooked for the position.

Because building rapport is so important, understanding the different types of interviewers you will encounter and adapting your communication style to meet their expectations will increase your chances of being offered the job. One way to anticipate an interviewer's style is by researching an organization's culture before the meeting. Corporate culture can be broken down into two main categories: conservative culture and social culture.

Culture	Characteristics
Conservative culture	This type of organization has most likely been around for a long time and has firm, effective processes in place There may not be a lot of diversity among employees or upper management All corporate policies and procedures are clearly communicated to employees in writing so everyone is aware of what is expected of them; this no-nonsense approach may attract the Just the Facts Ma'am interviewer (see page 72)
Social culture	This type of organization most likely encourages a team-oriented environment in which there is a lot of open communication between peers and management Creative ideas are welcomed to improve operations, affect bottom line results, and improve customer relations; this flexible business approach may attract the Chatterbox interviewer (see page 73)

Please note that the chart serves simply as a guide. Regardless of the corporate culture, you should be prepared to manage all types of interviewer styles, including the Uh Duh interviewer (see page 75).

You can find out about an organization's culture by setting up informational interviews (see Chapter 4) or by conducting company research (see page 95).

JUST THE FACTS MA'AM INTERVIEWER

The Just the Facts Ma'am interviewer will most likely skip the idle chitchat and begin asking interview questions right away. The Just the Facts Ma'am bases his or her hiring decision on how closely your background matches the job description, so expect pointed questions.

HOW TO SAY IT

- The interviewer will be interested in hearing examples, facts, and data. For example, making a vague statement such as, *"I'm a profit-driven, quality-focused operations leader who has experience in driving internal growth and leading startup and turnaround efforts,"* won't impress the Just the Facts Ma'am interviewer. However, a specific answer such as this will earn brownie points: *"As the director of strategic marketing for China Amusement Park, I launched a theme park within a brand-new market that achieved 100 percent of its attendance goals within the first four months of operation and 80 to 100 percent brand awareness in Asia-Pacific markets."*

Advantages

- The interviewer will be very thorough and ask relevant questions throughout the interview. For this reason, you will have a strong sense of the job requirements and what is expected of you by the end of the interview.
- Since the interviewer is interested in what you have achieved, you will have the opportunity to talk about your greatest accomplishments.
- If you don't answer a question fully, the interviewer may ask for additional information giving you an opportunity to reanswer the question.

Disadvantages

- Because the interviewer is all business, her demeanor may come off as cold or harsh. But in reality, the interviewer may not be either. She simply sees the interview as a business meeting and adapts a straightforward approach. This may make for an unintentionally uncomfortable interview setting.
- The interviewer will take full control of the interview, making it difficult to participate in a two-way conversation.
- The interviewer may not display emotion, and you may leave the interview wondering if you made a positive impression.

CHATTERBOX INTERVIEWER

The Chatterbox decision maker is enthusiastic, friendly, and animated. Her hiring decision will be heavily influenced by intuition, making your experience and achievements secondary considerations. The interview may seem like a social event rather than a business meeting.

HOW TO SAY IT

- Since the Chatterbox interviewer likes to talk, ask a lot of questions regarding the company to encourage him to discuss relevant issues. (See Chapter 13 for questions to ask interviewers.)
- Your answers should be warm, personal, and delivered with an enthusiastic tone of voice. Try to be as laid-back as you can, without letting your guard down.
- The interviewer will likely go off on irrelevant tangents, but don't interrupt her. Instead, look for opportunities to include relevant information about your background. For example, making a statement such as, *"Ms. Cohen, the story you just shared with me reminded me of the time I worked for ABC Corporation and I was challenged to . . ."* will work very well.

WHAT NOT TO SAY

- Don't provide too many facts; offer just enough to keep the interviewer informed of your abilities. For example, suppose the Chatterbox interviewer asks, *"How do you stay current on industry trends?"* Make a statement such as, *"I stay abreast of industry trends by continuing my education. In fact, I recently became a Certified Insurance Service Representative, and I am in the process of obtaining the Certified Insurance Consultant designation."* This short answer provides the interviewer exactly what she needs to know regarding your commitment to the industry.

Advantages

- The interview setting will be pleasant, and you may not feel interview anxiety—allowing you to enjoy the experience.
- The interviewer may volunteer information regarding candidates who have interviewed for the position, allowing you to compare and adjust your answers to suit the interviewer's expectations.

Disadvantages

- Since the interviewer may engage in a lot of small talk, you may leave the interview without a strong sense of the job requirements.
- You may let your guard down in such a casual interview setting and divulge information that will hinder your chances of receiving a job offer.
- You may follow the interviewer's lead and go off on tangents discussing topics that are irrelevant to the open position.

UH DUH INTERVIEWER

The Uh Duh interviewer is an inexperienced interviewer who may read from a list of canned questions and rarely look up from his notes. The interviewer may be visibly nervous and will want the interview to end quickly.

HOW TO SAY IT

- Though it's important to enter every interview with a solid understanding of your key selling points, it's even more important when dealing with a novice interviewer because it may be up to you to fill in the gaps of silence—should there be any. To break the silence you can say, *"You will be interested in my experience in . . ."*
- The interviewer may not be able to make a smooth transition from one question to the next. You can help keep the conversation running smoothly by ending some of your responses with a question. For example, *"Considering my response to your question, do my qualifications match your requirements?"*

Advantages

- You'll be able to set the agenda by making statements such as, *"Mr. Dobbs, let's take a look at my résumé and the points I highlighted under . . ."*
- If you lack the necessary experience but are able to put the interviewer at ease, he may evaluate your suitability on your interpersonal and communication skills rather on the technical aspects of the job. Therefore, make it a point to be a talkative and active participant.

Disadvantages

- It may be up to you to take control of the interview. You can't allow the interviewer's nervousness to be contagious. If you allow yourself to be on edge, the interview may not run smoothly.

- The interviewer may not provide enough information regarding company benefits or job requirements, and you may leave the interview without enough knowledge to make an educated decision on whether you want the job.

PART III

Winning Answers to the Most Common Interview Questions

7

Preparing Original Answers to Typical Questions

Employers expect candidates to enter an interview prepared with answers to potential questions, but applicants can quickly draw criticism if they provide overrehearsed or canned responses to questions that are meant to give the interviewer an accurate picture of the candidate's true accomplishments.

It's easy to fall into the trap of unintentionally giving canned answers, especially when you're feeling pressured to respond perfectly and impress the interviewer. Don't be fooled by the following interview misconceptions that often lead to generic, disappointing answers:

- ***The interviewer has a specific candidate in mind and you won't be considered for the position if you don't fit the predetermined mold.*** This misinformation often causes candidates to provide an-

swers they believe the interviewer wants to hear rather than responding to a question honestly.
Reality: Though it is true that interviewers have an ideal candidate in mind, that doesn't mean they aren't open to hearing what you have to offer. After all, you were invited to interview because you piqued the interviewer's interest. Rather than trying to fit into a mold, demonstrate the qualities you have to offer that other candidates may lack. Doing so will make your responses unique and allow you to stand apart from the crowd.

- ***Responses need to be short or the interviewer will lose interest.*** This myth leads applicants to provide vague snippets of their qualifications such as, *"I'm a hard worker"* or *"I'm a perfectionist"* in fear that detailed responses will bore the interviewer.
Reality: Interviewers are interested in learning about your background and qualifications. If you draw on your experiences, you will impress the interviewer with the originality of your responses.

HOW TO STEER CLEAR OF CANNED RESPONSES

You will never impress an interviewer with canned responses, so always do your best to answer questions with original, specific information that directly reflects your own experience and goals. Preparing answers to common interview questions ahead of time is the key to providing thoughtful answers. Here are some ways to anticipate possible questions based on your industry and the position you're applying for:

- **Participate in informational interviews.** As mentioned in Chapter 4, participating in informational interviews is crucial for preparing effectively for an interview. While attending informational interviews, ask about the types of questions you can expect during a job interview and the types of responses an interviewer may be looking for. Using the information you gather, prepare answers to potential interview questions.
- **Participate in mock interviews.** To practice, ask a friend or hire a Certified Interview Coach to videotape a mock interview. Prepare for this interview as you would prepare for a real interview and groom and dress appropriately. During the sessions, you will be able to practice giving responses to potential interview questions and become more comfortable with the thought of interviewing. After the mock interview, rate your interview performance and answers by highlighting your strengths and the areas that need improvement.
- **Use job descriptions.** To pinpoint the key skills and personal attributes employers are looking for, take the time to review job descriptions in your field. Once you have gathered job descriptions that interest you, underline the relevant experiences and personal traits that appear in the job description. Then formulate potential questions you may be asked based on the skills required. Job descriptions can be found on online job boards. (See page 90 for example questions based on job descriptions.)

THE BUILDING BLOCKS OF EVERY INTERVIEW QUESTION

The idea of preparing original answers to potential interview questions can become intimidating when you begin to imagine the countless approaches interviewers can take when developing their lists of questions for you.

The good news is that no matter how endless the questioning possibilities may seem, all questions asked during an interview ultimately tap into the following areas:

- *Adaptive skills*. These are traits that will enable you to adapt to most working environments. For example, being dependable, team-oriented, and self-confident are traits that can be used in all industries and professions.
- *Transferable skills*. These are skills that are not specific to one job and can easily translate in any position and company. For example, communication skills, attention to detail, and organizational skills can be easily transferred to a new position.
- *Job-related skills*. These are competencies that are specific to an occupation and are often attained through training, education, and experience. For example, an administrative assistant's job-related skills may include clerical and computer capabilities.

Almost any question that comes your way will be linked to one of these skill categories. As preparation for interviewing, take the time to list your adaptive, transferable, and job-related skills and write down how each of these skills will benefit a hiring organization. Doing this exercise will allow you to pinpoint your most impressive qualifications before the interview and help you prepare answers to traditional and behavioral-style interview questions.

TRADITIONAL INTERVIEW QUESTIONS

The most common interview questions are usually structured as either closed or open ended, leaving it up to you to provide as much or as little supporting information as you'd like when giving your response.

- Closed-ended questions technically require a only a yes or no response and may begin with a phrase such as these: *"Do you have experience in . . . ," "Are you familiar with . . . ,"* and *"Have you ever . . ."*
- Open-ended questions require you to elaborate on your responses but don't request specific details (it is up to you to choose a relevant answer based on your instincts and experiences). These questions may begin with one of these phrases: *"What exposure have you had with . . . ," "What would you do if . . . ," "What is the most important . . . ,"* and *"How would you handle . . ."*

Advantage

- Open-ended questions are generally hypothetical, allowing you to answer with an explanation of what you would do if faced with the specified situation without requiring you to have related experience. That said, if you do have experience in the area, let the interviewer know. If asked, *"What would you do if you were confronted with an upset customer?"* you can answer one of the following ways:

Experience	Sample Script
No experience	*"If I were confronted with an upset customer, I would satisfy the customer's needs without violating company policies."*
With experience	*"As part of my job with Imperial Imports, I maintain strong relationships with customers. Occasionally, a customer becomes upset due to servicing issues. When that happens I take the time to listen to the customer's concerns, sympathize, and direct him to the appropriate department."*

Disadvantages

- You may be nervous and find it difficult to elaborate on close-ended questions, leaving it up to the interviewer to fill in the gaps and come up with his own conclusions.
- When asked open-ended questions you may begin to ramble because you aren't exactly sure which experience you should highlight. This may result in incoherent responses.

HOW TO SAY IT

- When presented with a closed-ended question, it can be tempting to provide just a yes or no response. But you should treat closed-ended questions as open-ended ones and elaborate. For example, you can answer the close-ended question, *"Do you have experience with Microsoft Excel?"* in the following ways:

Experience	Sample Script
No experience	*"I'm familiar with Microsoft Word and Access. In fact, I use both programs on a daily basis to create reports for management. Since I'm familiar with such programs, I'm sure I'll be able to pick up Excel with ease."*
With experience	*"Yes, I have worked with Microsoft Excel and have extensive experience creating formulas, functions, macros, and reusable templates."*

WHAT NOT TO SAY

- Never say just, *"I don't know," "No,"* or *"Yes"* when asked a question. This doesn't mean that you should exaggerate the truth regarding your experience, but it does mean that you should find something in your background that is relevant to what the interviewer is seeking.

BEHAVIORAL-STYLE INTERVIEW QUESTIONS

Behavioral-style interview questions allow the interviewer to assess if you have hands-on experience with the responsibilities outlined in the job description. The interviewer will have a clear agenda and will be looking for specific responses on how you handle common situations that occur on the job. The questions will begin with, *"Tell me about a time when . . . ," "Describe an instance of . . ." "Think about a circumstance when . . ."* and *"Tell me how you approached a situation in which . . ."*

Behavioral-style questions are similar to traditional open-ended questions, but in this case the interviewer is making an assumption that the candidate has experience in a specific area. For example, the behavioral-style question, *"Tell me about a time when you were approached by an upset customer"* requires the candidate to describe a specific scenario. On the other hand, an open-ended question such as, *"How would you handle upset customers?"* doesn't necessarily require the candidate to respond with a who, what, where, and when. The other major difference between traditional interview questions and behavioral-style questions is that behavioral questions are never phrased in a hypothetical manner. They always require you to give a specific answer based on your experiences.

Behavioral-style interview questions have become quite common over the years, and their popularity will increase as more interviewers realize that storytelling is the best method for gauging a candidate's future success. This type of interview format allows recruiters to shrink the candidate pool and effectively determine the keepers. For this reason, human resource representatives are investing in specialized training in the behavioral-based interview method.

Advantages

- There are no guessing games because the questions reveal the core competencies the job requires and the specific duties you will perform. For example, if the interviewer is asking questions regarding your customer service experience, it is easy to deduce that the job will require you to maintain customer relations.

- If you aren't answering questions fully, the interviewer will most likely ask follow-up questions such as, *"What happened next?" "What was the result?"* or *"Who else was involved in the project?"*—giving you an opportunity to provide the information the interviewer is seeking.

Disadvantage

- If you don't have the hands-on experience the company is seeking, it will be difficult to answer the questions.

HOW TO SAY IT

- When answering a behavioral-style question, use the STAR technique:
    - *Situation or Task.* Describe the context for the interviewer, including the name of the company, description of the project, and the team involved in solving the problem (if there was one).
    - *Action.* Describe the action that was taken and explain the reason behind your chosen strategy.
    - *Result.* Describe the outcome. Was the primary objective met? What did you learn from the experience?
- Elaborate and provide answers that are at least one to two minutes long.

WHAT NOT TO SAY

- If asked a question concerning an area you don't have experience in, don't say, *"I've never encountered that situation."* Instead, answer hypothetically. For example, if asked, *"Tell me about a time when you had to solve a problem for which there were no rules to follow,"* a good response would be, *"I have a strong ability to overcome obstacles and think independently. If I were presented with a problem to solve that had no set rules, I would brainstorm solutions and use my experience in the field to come up with viable options. This strategy will allow me to make decisions based on practical business sense and not impulsive, emotional reactions."*

DEVELOPING POTENTIAL INTERVIEW QUESTIONS

Now that you know the basic makeup of an interview question, you can create a rather accurate list of potential questions that you might encounter at your next interview. As discussed at the beginning of the chapter, scanning relevant job descriptions is a great starting point.

Use the following sample job description for a marketing assistant to develop potential interview questions:

> The successful candidate <u>will produce marketing collateral</u> (e.g., brochures, web content, trade show booth creation, press releases, monthly newsletter distribution) that supports the organization's existing brand. <u>Excellent copy writing skills</u> and hands-on <u>knowledge of graphic programs</u> such as Adobe Illustrator, Pagemaker, and Photoshop is required. Must be a <u>team player</u>; be <u>creative</u>, <u>driven</u>, <u>personable</u>, and <u>professional</u>; and have a degree or training in marketing.

Job Requirements	Traditional Interview Questions	Behavioral-Based Interview Questions
Job related: Write press releases	Do you have experience writing press releases?	Tell me about a time you wrote a press release that garnered positive media attention.
Adaptive skill: Team player	Do you like to work independently or as part of a team?	Describe a circumstance in which working as a team produced better results than if you had worked on the project independently.
Transferable skill: Creative	How would your peers describe your creativity?	Tell me about a time when you came up with an innovative idea that was adopted by your department.

As you can see, job descriptions hold a wealth of information that you can use to your advantage when preparing for an interview.

Though it is nearly impossible to determine the exact questions that will be asked during an interview, being aware of the types of questioning techniques interviewers will use and developing potential questions that may be asked are valuable resources to have at your disposal. To assist you in preparing for interview questions, the forthcoming chapters cover typical interview questions and sample responses you can review to create your own answers.

8

Will You Fit In? Interview Questions

When you consider that most employees resign or are fired due to personality clashes, it's no wonder that your interaction with coworkers, direct reports, and customers are the driving forces behind your career's success.

Interviewers will evaluate your interpersonal skills to determine how well you would fit in as a member of their team. Keep in mind that effective interaction goes beyond being friendly. Those with strong interpersonal skills (1) have an ability to build rapport with others instantly, (2) demonstrate active listening by focusing on the speaker's message during a conversation rather than tuning them out to plan what they will say next, (3) read people and adapt their communication styles to that of the listeners, and (4) know how to gain cooperation and get their point across without alienating others.

Interviewers will assess your interpersonal skills by asking "will you fit in" questions in the following categories:

- Why us?
- How are your communication skills?
- Are you manageable?
- Are you a team player?
- Are you an effective manager?

WHY US?

Savvy job seekers make their decisions to interview with companies after conducting thorough research. This is because they know that not all companies are the same—even if they sell the same product or service.

You will find that all companies you interview with will have a different mission, operating procedures, and traditions that directly influence the overall makeup of the company and its employees' day-to-day practices. Common variations include these:

- Whether the company encourages professional development and allows employees to enroll in classes to keep their skills up to date.
- The company's dress code and whether employees are expected to wear corporate or casual dress.
- Whether there is a we vs. them mentality when it comes to employee and management relations.
- Perks employees receive such as subsidized daycare, bagel Fridays, and an in-house gym or any other benefits geared to making employees feel valued.
- Whether employees are expected to work overtime or on weekends.

Company Research Questions

Interviewers are impressed by the initiative and enthusiasm of candidates who have taken the time to find out about the company before the interview. Below is a list of questions you should find the answers to when researching a hiring organization.

- What is the overview of the company, including its history and image?
- Is the company public, private, or nonprofit?
- Is the company economically stable?
- What is its size (employees, revenue)?
- What is the past and projected growth rate?
- What is its position in the marketplace including its key competitors?
- What is the demand for the products and services?
- Who are its customers?
- How is it structured (divisions, subsidiaries)?
- What is the corporate culture/style of the company?
- What is the organization's management style?
- What is the environment/politics of the company?
- Who are the key decision makers?
- Where is it located? Is it national or global?
- Who are its competitors?
- What are the potential opportunities and pitfalls?

Source: Elaine Dryer, Coaching Passages

To find answers to these questions, you can use the following resources to discover company information.

Online Resources

- **America's Career InfoNet.** The "Employer Locator" on this website lets you search for company information by occupation, industry, and location. *www.acinet.org/acinet/employerlocator/employerlocator.asp*

- **Company website.** By visiting the hiring organization's website, you are likely to find information about its mission, products/services, and the management team.
- **CNN Money.** You will be able to find valuable information on publicly traded companies including financial statements, stock information, and annual revenue. *http://money.cnn.com/news/companies*
- **Bloomberg Online Magazine.** This site provides the latest in company news and financial information. *www. bloomberg.com*
- **Hoover's Online.** This site provides company overviews, financial information, information on key people, and top competitors. *www.hoovers.com/free*
- **PR Newswire.** Search the site for company press releases. *www.prnewswire.com*

Offline Resources

- **Company newsletters.** If you know someone who works for the company you are interested in, ask her if she can supply you with a company newsletter. This is a great resource for finding the latest information on a company and learning tidbits that will provide insight on the company's culture. For example, if you find that the newsletter contains information on the employee of the month or statistics of the company baseball team, you can infer that the organization values its people.
- **Marketing collateral (brochures, informational packets).** The information you find in these materials will provide insight on the company's products.

- **Informational interviews.** See Chapter 4 for what you can learn during an informational interview.

Company research will allow you to decide whether a company is the right fit for you on a professional and a personal level. Once you believe that a company is a good fit, you will have the basis for your answer when asked why-us questions.

HOW TO SAY IT

- Cite company facts you gleaned from research to reinforce your interest in working for the organization.
- Discuss how your personality and accomplishments will be an added value to the organization.
- Tell the interviewer how your personal and professional interests align with the company's mission or standard practices.
- To demonstrate interest, ask the interviewer questions. (See Chapter 13 for sample questions you can ask.)

Company Characteristics

conservative
cutting edge
established
groundbreaking
industry leader
innovative
pioneering
social
traditional
well-known

Power Phrases

built your reputation on employees' needs
challenging place to work
deliver competitive services
economically viable
encourage competitive team spirit
maintain a high level of standard
pattern of sustained growth
recognized as an industry leader
superior workplace environment

Sample Why-Us Interview Questions and Answers

- **What do you know about our company?**
  - The only way to prepare for this question is to conduct company research. Learn as much as you can about the company's services and products so you can highlight the reason(s) the organization appeals to you. When answering this question, it isn't necessary to provide a laundry list of reasons—one will suffice. Of course, if there are many reasons then feel free to elaborate on a few of the key points without going overboard.
  - **How to Say It:** *"I took the liberty of reviewing your corporate website before submitting my résumé for consideration. I was drawn to the fact that you are a family-owned business because I like the warm, friendly yet professional atmosphere that a family-owned business has. Since most people spend more time at work than with their families, it's important to have a working environment that is inviting."*

- **What other companies are you interviewing with?**
  - Avoid supplying specific company names and getting too involved in discussing the pros and cons of other companies you are interviewing with. You want the conversation to be focused on you and the open position and not on the interviewer's competition. For this reason, briefly provide generic information (i.e., company reputation, size, annual revenue, or the number of employees) and focus the bulk of your response on the appealing attributes of the company you are interviewing with.
  - **How to Say It:** *"I'm selective and choose to interview with companies that are leaders and well respected in the field. Those are exactly the reasons I am drawn to your organization. I've been following the recent expansion of your organization and am impressed by the level of commitment demonstrated toward employees and customers."*
- **What prompted you to apply for a position within our company?**
  - The interviewer will want to know if you conducted company research before you submitted your résumé or if you blindly applied to every open position you qualify for. For this reason, focus your response on the aspects of the organization that piqued your interest (e.g., their products/services or reputation).
  - **How to Say It:** *"While conducting research on your company, I read through the information on the company's website and was intrigued by the new pharma-*

ceutical drugs pending FDA approval. The prescription drugs your company is looking to introduce to the public will have a significant effect on the health of patients with terminal cancer. As a pharmaceutical sales representative for your company, I would enthusiastically promote this innovative product."

- **How does this company compare to other companies you have worked for?**
  - The proper way to answer this question is to focus on the positive attributes of the hiring organization, without making negative comments regarding previous employers.
  - **How to Say It:** *"It's not a secret that the economy has been sluggish for the last few years, and I've worked for companies that were forced to downsize their labor forces as a way to cut costs. From my company research, I noticed that your company has remained strong in turbulent times due to proactive measures. You're always looking to implement the best practices to ensure you stay ahead of the curve. With my ability to cultivate new accounts and your company's good public standing, I'm convinced we can penetrate the market."*
- **Why do you want to work for our organization?**
  - The interviewer asks this question to gauge your interest in working specifically for her organization. For this reason, focus your response on the attributes of the company that made it stand apart from other potential employers. That said, stay away from bringing up benefits that may be construed as self-centered such as salary or company

perks. Instead, mention the company culture, organizational management style, its mission statement, or any other particulars that caught your eye during your research.

- **How to Say It:** *"In my search for the right company fit, I went on numerous informational interviews. The name of your company was mentioned quite a few times as one I should pursue a career with. Based on the recommendations made by others, I took the time to research your company's history. I liked what I learned. Specifically, that the company donates 10 percent of all proceeds to animal rights organizations. I've been an animal lover all my life and am known to take in strays. This company would be a wonderful place to be a part of—a company that is conscious of the environment and those who inhabit it."*
- **How to Say It:** *"During the job fair at UCLA, I met with two recruiters from your organization. I was immediately struck by their level of enthusiasm for the company and knew this is a great organization to work for. I submitted my résumé for consideration and am pleased that I have the opportunity to interview for the accounting entry-level position."*

- **What skills have you honed in previous positions that will benefit this organization?**
  - Chances are there are other qualified candidates applying for the position so it's important to inform the interviewer of your unique characteristics. Take the time to mention your notable accomplishments or mention areas in your professional life that you are most proud of.

- **How to Say It:** *"I'm proficient in all phases of the sales cycles—from prospecting, presentations, negotiations, closing, and follow-up. Through these skills, I've successfully exceeded goals for my previous employer, Moonbeam Microsystems. With my strong background in relationship building, I'm certain that I'll be able to bring the same results to your organization."*
- **How to Say It:** *"During my college career I worked part-time for Community Bank. Part of its two-week training consisted of establishing a strong team environment to accomplish goals. Working for this national bank is where I learned the importance of being a cooperative team player and this is a skill I can easily transfer into a position within your company."*

- **Why do you believe you can make an effect on our organization?**
  - Wanting to work for an organization and being qualified to work for them are two different things. The interviewer wants to know why they should hire you. When answering this question, take inventory of how your experiences can benefit the company.
  - **How to Say It:** *"Since I grew up and was educated in this school district, I understand the culture of the neighborhood and can identify with the issues families are experiencing. With this keen understanding, I believe I can gain student, parent, and community trust. This will enable me to be an effective teacher and motivator in the classroom."*

HOW ARE YOUR COMMUNICATION SKILLS?

In almost every job description, you will find that the open position requires the applicant to have excellent communication skills. This is because interviewers want to be certain that you are capable of communicating your thoughts effectively to maintain relations and inform others of your ideas.

HOW TO SAY IT

- Through your responses, demonstrate that you have an adaptive communication style and that you can interact with individuals of all levels. From clients who are in need of information regarding the company's products or services to business associates with whom you network to get referrals, to vendors with whom you negotiate to get the best prices, and team members with whom you effectively collaborate on projects.
- Let the interviewer know that you know which type of communication is needed for each situation that comes up. For example, e-mail or memos can be used for quick, informal messages; in-person conversations can take place when critical items are brought to your attention; phone calls can be used to check on clients' satisfaction; and postal letters can be used for formal correspondence, such as contracts.

Power Words

advised
announced
answered
broadcasted
circulated
collaborated
compromised
connected
contacted
conveyed
cooperated
corresponded
counseled
directed
deliberated
disclosed
disseminated
distributed
exposed
informed
interacted
notified
planned
proposed
publicized
published
reasoned
recommended
related
reported
revealed
shared
simplified
stated
suggested
updated

Personal Characteristics

accessible
active listener
approachable
articulate
assertive
believable
coherent
collaborative
communicative
confident
congenial
considerate
convincing
cordial
credible
diplomatic
discreet
effectual
expressive
eloquent
flexible
impressive
influential
insightful
lucid
open-minded
perceptive
personable
persuasive
polished
polite
refined
self-assured
stimulating
tactful
well-spoken

Power Phrases

ability to simplify complex issues
accurately assess and react positively during difficult discussions
advanced oral communication skills
courteous and respectful of other's opinions
encourage healthy debate
gain the trust of customers
instantly build rapport with business associates
interact effectively
manage confidential correspondences
portray a persuasive, confident demeanor
project professionalism
provide detailed updates on project activities
provide effective conflict resolution techniques
select the appropriate words to get my message across
share information with upper management
sought-after motivational speaker
successfully mediated
tactful and diplomatic communicator

Sample Communication Skills Interview Questions and Answers

- **How do you communicate with stakeholders regarding the status of ongoing projects?**
  - Focus your response on your ability to build credibility and trust with vendors, the board of directors, management, and coworkers by maintaining a clear line of communication with them at all times.
  - **How to Say It:** *"As a project manager, I keep stake-*

holders in the loop by providing detailed status reports—outlining projects that have been completed and those that are still in progress. In addition, I lead monthly meetings with stakeholders to answer any questions they may have and bring everyone up-to-date on the latest activities."

- **Describe how your written communication skills help you achieve desired results.**
    - Effective written communication is part of daily exchanges in a work environment. When answering this question, mention your ability to develop persuasive, clear, and concise correspondence.
    - **How to Say It:** *"I am called on to use written communication skills in my everyday interactions within the office—from simple messages such as e-mail to more complex and detailed reporting such as business proposals. I am well equipped to communicate in a variety of ways and have used my skills to increase efficiency within my department."*
    - **How to Say It:** *"While earning my degree, I worked part-time in an entry-level position in public relations. I received hands-on training in writing promotional pieces for inclusion in the local newspaper. I learned how to create compelling copy, and I can easily transfer this skill into a full-time position as a public relations assistant."*
- **How do you avoid misunderstandings in the workplace?**
    - If ignored, misunderstandings can snowball into an unmanageable situation. When answering this question, demonstrate your capability of addressing delicate situations effectively.

 - **How to Say It:** *"When communicating, we are judged by others' perceptions, and not necessarily by our intentions. When I encounter a situation in which I have been misunderstood, I rephrase my sentiments and quickly clarify any miscommunication with openness and honesty. I find that dealing with the situation head-on allows us to focus on the task at hand."*

- **Tell me about a time when your communication skills were recognized by management.**
  - Discuss a time when you received a letter of praise for effectively handling a sensitive situation or received a pat on the back for maintaining a professional demeanor under less than desirable circumstances.
  - ***How to Say It:*** *"Originally I was hired as a customer service representative, and I was charged with handling consumer inquiries. Within six months, the position of customer service manager became available, and I was approached by the head of the department to interview for the position. She said she noticed how I managed customer concerns with diplomacy and that my communication style could easily transfer into a management role. I interviewed for the position, received the job offer, and readily accepted the position."*

ARE YOU MANAGEABLE?

The hiring manager will be extremely interested to know if you need to be micromanaged, if you will you go against the status quo and ruffle feathers, or if you are able to work independently and apply constructive criticism to improve your work performance.

HOW TO SAY IT

- Demonstrate your ability to perform your job with little or no supervision through examples of successful independent work you've done in the past.
- Make it a point to express that you respect your manager's role and are motivated to do what it takes to help her succeed.
- Communicate your ability to follow instructions and corporate policies and guidelines.

WHAT NOT TO SAY

- Don't share harsh words regarding current or past corporate policies and procedures or regarding your current or previous manager because doing so will leave the interviewer with the impression that you have a negative attitude.

Power Words

accommodated
achieved
adapted
assisted
brainstormed
carried out
collaborated
complemented
complied
contributed
cooperated
enhanced
executed
exercised judgment
facilitated
implemented
improved
incorporated
initiated
participated in
performed
prevented
provided
solved
streamlined
supported
volunteered

Personal Characteristics

accommodating
accomplished
accountable
approachable
attentive
committed
communicative
competent
conscientious
considerate
consistent
cooperative
courteous
dedicated
dependable
devoted
efficient
experienced
focused
friendly
hardworking
motivated
multitasker
open to change
patient
proactive
punctual
receptive
reliable
respectful
responsive
supportive
team player
trouble-shooter
well-rounded

Power Phrases

able to follow instructions
adhere to policies and procedures
approachable, engaging personality
believe in the company's vision
dependable team player
entrusted by senior executives
flexible, adaptable work style
follow company rules and regulations
recognized as a contributing team member
support the vision of the department
welcome constructive feedback
willing to learn and adapt to new situations
work in partnership

Sample Are You Manageable Interview Questions and Answers

- **Describe an instance in which your current or previous manager could have done a better job in managing you.**
  - Avoid making negative comments—even if you have ill feelings surrounding your current or previous supervisor's management style. Instead, briefly touch on any misunderstanding and focus the majority of the response on the positive outcome.
  - **How to Say It:** *"When I was hired by XYZ Systems, I replaced an employee who failed to complete his assignments on time. As a result, his progress needed to be closely monitored to ensure deadlines were met. Being used to micromanaging the efforts of my predecessor, my supervisor checked in often to make certain I was on track. Eventually, she realized that I have a strong work ethic and could be depended on to successfully complete assigned tasks. She mentioned several times that she appreciated my work style because it made her job easier."*
- **Tell me about a time when you disagreed with your supervisor on how to complete a task. What was the result?**
  - It's no secret that it's virtually impossible to always see eye to eye with management. So the interviewer isn't seeking a "I never disagreed with my supervisor" type of response. In fact, if you did respond in that manner, the interviewer may conclude that you are a follower and not a leader. When

answering this question, focus your response on how you effectively communicate with your manager when there is a difference in opinion.

- ***How to Say It:*** *"At ABC Company, the manager implemented a hardball approach to managing accounts payable. The new procedure called for customers to pay their invoices within thirty days or forfeit their rights to order more products until their accounts were up to date. I understood my manager's stance because the accounts payable department as a whole collected less than 50 percent of invoices on time. However, my personal collection averaged over 80 percent with our current sixty-day net. I was concerned that my customers would begin going to our competitors to fill their inventory. I approached my manager and respectfully voiced my thoughts. Ultimately, we went ahead with the manager's plan of action and agreed that I would keep a log of customer reactions. If the negative feedback was significant, we would revisit the issue. It was a great compromise."*

- **How would your current or previous employer describe your work ethic?**
  - An excellent way to gauge your manageability is by gaining insight on how others perceive your performance. When answering this question keep your response focused on the good qualities noticed by your previous or current manager.
  - **How to Say It:** *"My performance reviews have always been outstanding. In my most recent one, my manager indicated that my dependability and loyalty as an employee is evident by the fact that I always show up to*

work on time and, when needed, make myself available for overtime—making me an asset to the department."

- **How to Say It:** *"Throughout my college career, I worked as a retail associate for a merchant in the local mall. During my tenure, I collaborated with the assistant manager on how to cut costs and move merchandise. My manager always complimented me on my resourcefulness and dedication to the job."*

- **Name one characteristic that an effective manager holds.**
  - There isn't a right or wrong answer to this question. Before the interview, take the time to evaluate the qualities you find important in a manager. Choose the one that is most significant to you and stress it during the interview.
  - **How to Say It:** *"In one word,* trust. *Managers who trust their ability to manage, ultimately trust their team to carry out the responsibilities of the job with little or no supervision. In the end, trust enables managers to do their jobs, which is to develop new procedures and promote the direction of the department. Trust also empowers employees to be productive because they are aware management believes in their abilities."*

- **What kind of direction do you like to receive from your supervisor?**
  - Each supervisor has his or her own way of running a department, and this question is asked to determine if your needs match the current managing style. To answer this question, take note of the management style that suits you best. Do you like

minimal or a lot of direction? Do you like to have a manager who is hands on or hands off?

- **How to Say It:** *"My previous employers can attest to the fact that I'm an independent worker who successfully takes projects from cradle to grave. As a result, I perform my best when I receive clear expectations and guidelines and then am given the autonomy to complete the assignment."*
- **How to Say It:** *"My educational background coupled with my internship experience has prepared me for this type of work. That said, there are times when I do have questions and it's important to have a manager who has an open-door policy so I can ask questions as they arise."*

- **Describe the best boss you have ever had.**
  - There isn't a right or wrong answer to this question. Tell the interviewer the truth and provide the reason.
  - **How to Say It:** *"The best boss I ever had lead by example. Her belief in and passion for the company was contagious. Her style created an environment in which the department was motivated to perform well. It was truly a joy working for her."*
  - **How to Say It:** *"Between college semesters, I worked for KiddyCare Learning Center as a teacher's aide. The classroom teacher allowed me to create lesson plans and coordinate classroom plays. It was a pleasure working in an environment where I was encouraged to contribute ideas. That made me feel part of the team and that my opinion was valued."*

ARE YOU A TEAM PLAYER?

Whether your job requires you to work on projects with a team or sit behind a computer all day, team-player questions still apply. Interviewers want to know that if you work independently, you can still get along with others and not participate in gossip. On the other hand, if your position requires you to collaborate with others, they want to know you can do so seamlessly and cooperatively.

HOW TO SAY IT

- When approached with a team-player question, use words such as *we* instead of *I* to demonstrate that you excel in a cohesive, collaborative work environment.
- Demonstrate that you have an adaptable and flexible working style and easily fit into any work environment.

WHAT NOT TO SAY

- Even if you had negative experiences with working on a team, refrain from making negative comments.

Power Words

assisted	communicated	conceptualized
coached	completed	conducted
collaborated	complied with	conformed

contributed
cooperated
incorporated
initiated
produced
promoted
recommended
rectified
reinforced
resolved
selected
simplified
streamlined
strengthened
succeeded
suggested
supplied
supported

Personal Characteristics

achiever
active listener
adaptable
appreciative
committed
competent
conscientious
consistent
dedicated
dependable
detail-oriented
determined
diligent
disciplined
efficient
enthusiastic
flexible
go-getter
hard worker
loyal
passionate
persistent
positive
problem-solver
proficient
relational
reliable
resourceful
responsible
self-motivated
self-starter
supportive
tenacious
thorough
trustworthy
well-respected

Power Phrases

accept new challenges head on
actively participate
believe in joint, cooperative decision making
brainstorm for ways to make new ideas work
consider the effect of my actions on others
contribute to a productive work environment
contribute to company's long-term success

cooperative approach to achieving goals
dependably deliver
effectively collaborate to complete tasks
express thoughts responsibly
follow through on my commitments
foster trust and rapport
gain coworker buy-in
generate new ideas
go out of my way to assist team members
known as the office go-to person
maintain integrity
part of a cohesive team
play a proactive role
pool resources to get the job done
readily take on new challenges
readily take on unpopular tasks
thrive in a team-driven work environment
uncompromising work ethic
work late as needed
work together to accomplish goals

Sample Team Player Interview Questions and Answers

- **What has been your experience working in a team environment?**
  - When answering this question, make sure to reflect on the positive experiences you had in working in teams. Discuss skills you have gained or learned and/or ways in which you constructively contributed to a cohesive, collaborative environment.
  - **How to Say It:** *"Working in a team environment to achieve specific goals and targets has been a rewarding experience for me. My experiences collaborating with*

others has helped hone my communication skills and allowed me to refine the way I present ideas and interact with colleagues."

- **Describe how you would approach a team member who wasn't doing his part to complete a project.**
  - It's easy to collaborate in a team effort when everyone is working diligently toward the common goal. It's a different story altogether when you have to work with a coworker who isn't performing to expectations. The interviewer will want to know that you can approach an ineffective teammate with respect and professionalism.
  - **How to Say It:** *"It is rare to come across a team member who doesn't want to perform well. When a team member isn't pulling his weight, I think it's usually because he is having difficulty with a particular part of the project. Without putting the individual on the defensive, I would speak to him in private and ask if any assistance is needed. This approach wouldn't put the person on the defensive because I wouldn't be laying blame. Instead, I'd be offering to assist or clarify the parameters of the project."*

- **What is the number one ingredient that makes a team successful?**
  - To answer this question, reflect on teams that you have worked on in the past and stress the elements you enjoyed the most.
  - **How to Say It:** *"It's important for every team member to be committed to the project. A committed team will do all it can to complete the project on time and within the specified requirements. If roadblocks appear along*

the way, a committed team will brainstorm ideas on how to overcome the obstacle."

- **Are you competitive?**
  - Interviewers know that a healthy competitive spirit can lead to increased productivity, but at the same time, competitiveness can go too far and lead to a difficult work environment. The interviewer wants to know if you have drive coupled with a strong sense of team collaboration.
  - **How to Say It:** *"I'm competitive in the sense that I enjoy my work and like to see what I have accomplished at the end of the day. Although I'm competitive, I also like to see my coworkers succeed and if I can do something to make them successful, I will do so."*
  - **How to Say It:** *"Throughout my secondary and undergraduate career, I was actively involved in sports and learned the true meaning of sportsmanship—respect for oneself and team members. As a result, although I do consider myself competitive, it is complemented by my strong team-work skills."*

- **How would you characterize an effective team player?**
  - Based on your response, the interviewer will be able to determine the team-work skills you value and if maintaining respectful, professional, cooperative working relationships is important to you.
  - **How to Say It:** *"While working independently, a good team player gains great satisfaction from partnering with coworkers to solve problems and improve the quality of company services. For this reason, I enjoy contributing ideas and building on the thoughts of team members."*

- **How do you handle it when the department decides to go with someone else's idea and not yours?**
  - Do you pout? Do you try to sabotage the end result? Or are you cooperative? The interviewer wants to know if you are able to work with team members after a difference of opinion. Because the way disagreements are handled can affect team cohesiveness, the interviewer wants to determine if you handle conflicts maturely—not allowing them to spiral out of control.
  - **How to Say It:** *"I think a conflict-free work environment is one that lacks a diversified team. Different values and perceptions lead to innovative ideas and, ultimately, a more effective work environment. For this reason, I welcome different point of views and, regardless of whose idea is chosen, team members can count on me to complete my share of the workload."*

ARE YOU AN EFFECTIVE MANAGER?

Interviewers are seeking a manager who can direct reliable and efficient operations and motivate and train staff members. Every manager has her own way, and it's up to the interviewer to determine which management style fits best within the organization. To answer management questions effectively, determine your management style and become aware of your strengths and weaknesses.

HOW TO SAY IT

- A conservative company will be interested in a manager who has a directive management style and provides clear expectations to reduce the number of mistakes made.

- A social company will be interested in a manager with a participatory management style and who encourages team members to share their thoughts and contribute to the decision-making process.
- Regardless of the company you are interviewing with, your answers must demonstrate your ability to be a positive role model and to motivate team members to meet objectives.
- Managing the activities of others requires you to be an effective communicator. The interviewer will want to know that you will be able to provide encouragement when needed and constructive criticism when appropriate.

Power Words

administered
approved
assigned
authorized
coached
committed
created
defined
delegated
designated
directed
encouraged
enforced
established
executed
facilitated
generated
implemented
improved
influenced
initiated
instructed
integrated
involved
issued
led
maintained
managed
modified
motivated
overhauled
oversaw
produced
promoted
ran
reorganized

Personal Characteristics

accessible
action-oriented
active listener
approachable
articulate
balanced
charismatic
coach
communicative
conceptual
confident
consistent
dynamic
empathetic
empowering
encouraging
facilitator
flexible
focused
honest
insightful
inspiring
intelligent
objective
open-minded
passionate
perceptive
persistent
persuasive
proactive
reachable
sincere
straightforward
strategic thinker
supportive
tactful

Power Phrases

ability to see the big picture
assemble self-directed teams
assess employees' strengths and weaknesses
build a cohesive team
capture opportunities
direct the efforts of a sales team
drive organizational change
encourage staff development
ensure each employee knows what is expected
establish vision and direction
exceed productivity goals
facilitate team collaboration
flawlessly manage
implement policies and procedures
instrumental in developing new business model
integrate employee ideas
long-range strategic planning
lead cross-functional teams
maintain an open-door policy
manage conflict effectively

produce highly productive teams
provide constructive feedback
provide direction and vision
put together unified teams
reward staff members' efforts
select, manage, and train staff
strategic business sense
strengthen employee relations

Sample Are You an Effective Manager Interview Questions and Answers

- **Where do you think most managers fail and how is your approach different?**
  - To answer this type of question recall experiences you've had with poor managers. Describe what you observed and how your management style varies.
  - **How to Say It:** *"One of the primary responsibilities of a manager is to define parameters of a project, monitor the progress, and approach those not performing to standards. Most managers prefer to overlook poor performance to avoid making waves. I believe this approach stifles employee development, lowers the morale of productive team members, and robs the credibility of the manager. For this reason, I make it a point to provide feedback often to ensure corporate objectives are met."*
- **Think back to your worst manager. What did you learn from him or her?**
  - Resist the temptation to speak negatively. Choose your words carefully and focus your response on

what you learned from the experience as opposed to the manager's actions.

- **How to Say It:** *"Earlier in my career, I worked with a manager who excelled at putting out fires. I was really impressed by her calm demeanor when she managed pressing issues. Over time, I realized that most of the crises could have been avoided if she had set clear staff expectations from the onset. For this reason, I ensure all team members know their roles, and I create a supportive environment in which they feel safe to ask for clarification if needed."*

- **What is your biggest management mistake?**
  - Choose a mistake that you have overcome and that didn't have a detrimental effect on the department.
  - **How to Say It:** *"Earlier in my career, I believed I was more efficient than others and if I had to take the time to train someone I might as well complete the task myself. I quickly realized that proper delegation serves two purposes. The first is that it allows employees to strengthen their skills and contribute. Delegation also allowed me to spend more time overseeing projects instead of getting bogged down with details."*

- **How would you describe your management style?**
  - While conducting company research, you should be able to determine the organization's management style. Use the information you find to formulate a proper response. If you are unable to determine the organization's management style, simply share with the interviewer your style.
  - **How to Say It:** *"Adapting one style of management for every situation and employee rarely works. I've*

found that a flexible management style allows me to provide the most effective leadership for any situation that may arise. For example, in a time-critical situation, I use a directive style by which I provide team members with explicit instructions on how to execute a plan. On the other hand, when there is time to explore different options, I use a participatory style and encourage ideas from team members."

- **How do you handle conflict between two employees?**
    - Hard feelings among employees can affect their performances on the job, and sometimes that resentment can trickle down to others in the department—making the work environment uncomfortable and unproductive. For this reason, when answering this type of question, discuss your ability to address employee relations issues quickly and diplomatically.
    - **How to Say It:** *"When there is a personality conflict between employees, I hold a meeting with both parties present and allow each to provide a summary of his point of view. Once I've heard both sides, I ask how they propose the conflict be resolved. When a compromise has been reached, I get the employees to commit to the resolution."*

- **What was your biggest challenge you faced as a manager?**
    - If you've never been challenged the interviewer may infer you are a lazy manager who avoids conflicts and/or lets others do the problem solving. When answering this question, focus your response on the outcome instead of the challenge.

   - **How to Say It:** *"At Accounting Techs, Inc., I was promoted to management after serving as an accounting clerk for less than a year. This caused uneasiness among employees who felt slighted when I was selected for advancement. I realized that my success as a manager depended on whether I was able to engage the staff. I decided to hold a meeting to clarify that my role as the manager was to help them succeed—a role that I had unofficially taken on when I was a clerk, a role they were used to me having. After the meeting, team members were rejuvenated and excited about my leadership."*

- **Describe how you have made employees feel valued.**

   - Lack of acknowledgment is a reason employees resign. Your response should focus on employee-recognition programs you have implemented, the positive feedback you provide, or any other way you have made employees feel appreciated.
   - **How to Say It:** *"I introduced and presided over monthly power-hour meetings that provided a forum for employees to offer suggestions for improvements. Team members offered valuable insight that helped reduce the phone bill, improve vendor selection, and increase overall workplace efficiency. Through my experiences, I learned that employees feel valued by management when they see their recommendations implemented."*

- **Describe a time when you had to handle a high turnover rate.**

   - The interviewer may be asking this question for two reasons: (1) the company may be going through a high turnover rate and wants to know if you have experience giving a department a much needed face-lift and (2) the interviewer may want to know if you have had to handle a high turnover rate due to poor management skills. When answering this question keep in mind that high turnover rates are the result of poor management skills, and every time an employee resigns it costs the organization money, time, and resources. Being capable of slashing turnover rates will make you more appealing to the interviewer.

- **How to Say It:** *"When I started working for ABC Company, there was a high turnover rate due to disillusionment with management. The first initiative I took was to restore the lines of communication to begin developing trust. I accomplished this by instilling a true open-door policy by which employees were encouraged to share their concerns. This initiative worked swimmingly. As management we learned a lot from our employees, and we restructured corporate policies to reflect the needs of the organization and employees alike. In the end, the turnover rate was slashed 17 percent."*

9

Can You Do the Job? Interview Questions

Smooth talking and a sleek interview outfit can get you only so far in an interview. There will be a point when the interviewer will ask questions that will home in on your ability to do the job. He will want to make sure you are a productive employee who will contribute to the efficiency of the workforce. Your practical skills, reliability, ability to make sound decisions, and commitment will be evaluated.

To determine whether you are qualified and motivated to do your job well, interviewers will ask "can you do the job?" questions in the following categories:

- Job motivation and initiative
- Time management and organization
- Decision making and problem solving
- Creativity and innovation
- Presentation skills

JOB MOTIVATION AND INITIATIVE

Getting a hold of the technical aspect of a job is easy. What's more difficult is to perform tasks with enthusiasm. Lack of passion is easily detected by others, and it is often contagious. Customers notice and may decide to go to a competitor. Coworkers may notice and their work may suffer. Interviewers are aware of this, and they want to choose a new hire who has passion for her career.

HOW TO SAY IT

- Communicate your willingness to go beyond the specific job requirements to assist the organization in achieving its mission.
- Demonstrate enthusiasm for your career and discuss how your passion has translated into accomplishments that have benefited your current or previous employer.
- Recall a time when you made a suggestion that contributed to the growth, expansion, or productivity of a current or previous employer. Break down the reasons you were inspired to go the extra mile (e.g., management's style, corporate culture) and stress those motivating factors during the interview.

WHAT NOT TO SAY

- Be enthusiastic but don't sound overconfident and make statements such as, *"Oh, that sounds so simple. I can handle that."* Instead, be confident by stating, *"I had a similar experience at ABC Company, and the way I handled it was . . ."*

- Don't gush over the job but do show your sincere interest.

Power Words

accomplished
achieved
adhered
assessed
completed
conceived
contributed
created
designated
eliminated
evaluated
fielded
improved
initiated
maintained
mediated
oriented
participated
prepared
supported
worked

Personal Characteristics

committed
confident
determined
diligent
doer
dynamic
energized
enthusiastic
forward thinker
hard worker
loyal
persistent
progressive
resourceful
results-oriented
self-confident
self-motivated
self-starter
successful
tenacious
thorough

Power Phrases

acquire new knowledge through education
always give 100 percent
bring projects to completion
can be counted on to get the job done
commended for a strong work ethic
committed to excellence

consistently exceed manager's expectations
dedicated and hardworking professional
eager to learn new concepts
focused on achieving goals
high degree of integrity
institute sound judgment
perform effectively despite obstacles
put the plan in motion
recognized as an active, contributing team member
recognized as the go-to person
reputation for getting the job done
resourceful problem-solver
strong commitment to excellence
take pride in providing quality services

Sample Job Motivation and Initiative Interview Questions and Answers

- **If hired, how long do you plan to stay with us?**
  - No one knows what tomorrow will bring so it may be difficult to answer this question with a definitive answer. The safest answer is one that does not commit you to a specific time frame.
  - **How to Say It:** *"As long as I am making a significant contribution to the organization and growing professionally, I see myself making a long-term commitment."*
  - **How to Say It:** *"I had the same part-time job throughout college, while the other students would come and go. Provided that I am continually challenged, I expect to be as loyal and dependable for my next employer."*
- **Why did you pursue a career in . . . ?**
  - Discuss the reasons you were drawn to your profession. Don't get hung up on the right answer. Simply

speak from your heart and let the interviewer know what aspects of your job you truly enjoy.

- **How to Say It:** *"From an early age I knew I would dedicate my life to working with children. I thought of becoming a teacher or a social worker. I decided on teaching because I like the idea of providing a supportive and encouraging environment for children on a daily basis. I was also drawn to the creativity of the job; I welcome the opportunity to develop a curriculum that stimulates learning."*
- **How to Say It:** *"I started my college career without declaring a major because I wanted to keep my options open. I joined a number of college clubs and found that I was always drawn to the fund-raising committee. I like the tasks of fund-raising, including networking, sales, and marketing. There is so much variety in the field that I decided to dedicate my career to fund-raising for nonprofit organizations."*

- **What motivated you to search for another career opportunity?**
  - This question appears harmless, but it can damage your potential in a heartbeat if you're not careful. There are usually two reasons an individual embarks on a job search. The first is that there is a personality clash with a current manager. If this is the case, don't dwell on how much you dislike your boss. Keep your answer to this question as positive as possible. The interviewer wants to hire a team player, not a person who will bring negativity into the workplace. Another popular reason is the desire for professional growth. If this is this case, focus your

response on the reasons you believe you are ready to move up the corporate ladder.

  - **How to Say It:** *"After reviewing my present situation and career goals, I have determined that I don't have the opportunity to reach my highest potential. I have a strong background and dedication to delivering exceptional value to an employer's bottom line, and I'm exploring options that will allow me to perform at my best."*

- **Tell me about a job that wasn't the right fit. How did you stay motivated?**

  - Interviewers are aware that life is full of trial and errors, and they want to know how you handled an unfavorable situation. When answering this question focus less on the negatives of the job and more on what you learned.
  - **How to Say It:** *"When I was just out of college I accepted the first job offer I was given. I didn't take the time to figure out the type of company that best suited my work style. I quickly found that the organization wasn't the best fit. At the same time, I love the work that I do, so I didn't allow the company culture to affect my mood and the way I interacted with clients. After that experience, I've interviewed only with companies that match my work style. This is one of the reasons I applied for a position with your organization. From what I've read and heard here today, there is a mutual fit."*

- **You've been in this field for a long time. How do you avoid getting burned out?**

  - Because many people change careers frequently, the interviewer wants to be certain that your enthusiasm for the industry remains strong. When answering this question focus your response on the aspect of your job that stimulates you the most.

- **How to Say It:** *"I consider myself lucky to work in the human services field because I get paid to do what I love—help people be in a better place than they were yesterday. That's my motivation."*

- **How do you complete a task that you find boring?**
  - When answering this question, refrain from complaining about the tedious assignments you must execute. Instead, focus your response on your level of commitment to your job and the fact that you put in the same effort to every task you are assigned regardless of its nature.
  - **How to Say It:** *"I recognize that one task doesn't define my day or my job. I perform my least favorite tasks first thing so I can concentrate the rest of my day on areas that I enjoy."*

- **Why should I hire you?**
  - This question can be the defining moment of an interview. Take this opportunity to highlight the accomplishments you are most proud of. Draw on experiences in which you were instrumental in creating ideas, streamlining operations, and going beyond obvious solutions to improve the company's processes, bottom line, or public image.
  - **How to Say It:** *"As an account manager, I develop and maintain productive relationships that typically produce repeat and referral business. I do this by establishing a strong rapport with customers, so that both of us receive value from the relationship. If my clients encounter problems with my company's product or service,*

I act quickly to resolve the issue and retain their loyalty to the company. Based on my understanding of your requirements and my commitment to delivering excellent results, I am confident I can be a valuable contributing member of your team."

- **How to Say It:** *"While interning as a nurse in Community Hospital, I had the passion and drive to meet patients' expectations. I was dedicated to contributing to a safe, nurturing environment for those in recovery. I am positive I can bring that same level of enthusiasm to your facility."*

- **Tell me about a time when you went above and beyond what was expected of you.**
    - Focus your response on your initiative and your willingness to go the extra mile to meet customer expectations or to meet projected deadlines.
    - **How to Say It:** *"When I worked for People Against Domestic Violence, a family that was hearing impaired stayed at the safe house. Because they couldn't speak, it was difficult to communicate with them. In my spare time, I took the time to learn sign language so I could communicate with the family. They were very appreciative that I took the time to go inside their world, and management was impressed that I was able to communicate with the family and tend to their needs."*
    - **How to Say It:** *"Like me, most of the retail associates working at Children's Toys were college students. Whenever a team member had a paper or a test to study for, I would cover for him or her. Everyone knew that I could be counted on whenever I was needed."*

TIME MANAGEMENT AND ORGANIZATION

Employees fail to meet deadlines for two reasons: (1) lack of enthusiasm or confidence for the job, which leads to procrastination, and (2) poor organizational skills, which means extra time to complete tasks. Asking questions surrounding one's time management and organizational skills allows the interviewer to assess if you are able to set priorities and perform well in a deadline-driven environment.

HOW TO SAY IT

- To prepare for time management and organization interview questions, recall instances in which you effectively met a deadline. Identify the situation and the exact steps you took to ensure a positive outcome. This exercise will remind you of your ability to prioritize projects to meet proposed job targets.
- The interviewer will be assessing your ability to remain calm under pressure when overseeing multiple activities concurrently. For this reason, craft responses that demonstrate your ability to organize your workload so that you are not overwhelmed.
- Demonstrate how your enthusiasm for your work translates into your ability to hit the ground running when given assignments.

Power Words

allocated
analyzed
appointed
arranged
assembled
assessed
assigned
audited
balanced
broke down
calculated
categorized
classified
coordinated
delegated
designed
evaluated
examined
identified
indexed
mapped
modified
monitored
multitasked
organized
planned
prepared
prioritized
reassessed
reevaluated
reviewed
simplified
streamlined
structured
tabulated

Personal Characteristics

accurate
adaptive
comprehensive
conscientious
consistent
creative
detailed-oriented
diligent
effective
efficient
hardworking
identified
industrious
logical
meticulous
self-manager
thorough
productive
proficient
resourceful
well-organized

Power Phrases

allow flexibility in my workday
avoid postponing important tasks
balance work activities
break down tasks into manageable pieces

concentrate on one task at a time
control distractions that break my flow
divide a larger task into smaller ones
effectively manage daily interruptions
eliminate distractions
ensure sufficient time to complete tasks
establish a routine
evaluate assignments
focus gives direction
group similar tasks together
juggle multiple tasks
learned to say no
limit the time spent in meetings
make the most of my day
manage interruptions
organized workspace
plan, organize, and execute
prepare a daily to-do list
schedule meetings
set reasonable goals
set smarter objectives
start work activities right away
use a trusted system
use time in the most effective way possible

Sample Time Management and Organization Interview Questions and Answers

- **Describe the techniques you use to manage your time.**
  - Whether you choose to create a to-do list or tackle projects the moment they arrive on your desk, interviewers are aware that everyone has his own time management technique. For this reason, they won't be looking for a specific response. To answer this question, simply describe your method and why it works for you.
  - **How to Say It:** *"Instead of tackling projects on a first come, first serve basis, I evaluate each one that*

comes across my desk and rank it in terms of importance. This technique has worked very well for me. In fact, you will find that my desk isn't cluttered with incomplete projects or unresolved paperwork, because I make it a point to address issues as they arise and not wait until the last minute to manage my daily activities."

- **How to Say It:** *"As a college student, my days were filled with classes, campus activities, and a part-time job. To fulfill my responsibilities, I had to have strong time management skills. What worked for me was to set aside specific times for each activity. This structure allowed me to meet all my obligations on time."*

- **How do you ensure your day starts off on the right foot?**
  - Focus your response on your ability to arrange your day so that there are limited distractions and interruptions throughout your day.
  - **How to Say It:** *"I spend the last fifteen minutes of my day planning my goals for the next working day. I find this helps me unwind, and I'm able to get a jump start on the following day's activities. When I arrive to work the next day, I don't participate in morning rituals such as getting coffee, eating breakfast, and discussing what's for lunch with coworkers. I've observed such rituals take up at least thirty minutes every morning, making the workday begin at nine-thirty instead of nine. For this reason, I make it a point to go directly to my desk when I arrive to avoid getting sidetracked by non-work-related discussions."*

- **How to Say It:** *"Traditional methods are sometimes best. I start every morning with a three-mile run and eat a healthy breakfast. Treating myself well in the morning allows me to start my day off with a kick."*

- **How do you prioritize conflicting priorities?**
  - Because "I need it yesterday" is a common theme in workplace environments, focus your response on your ability to perform well under pressure when managing conflicting priorities.
  - **How to Say It:** *"I'm not one to get frazzled easily and believe that participating in more than one task is fun, challenging, and makes the day more interesting. When I have conflicting priorities, I set aside blocks of time for each to ensure all activities have my undivided attention. Then I dive right in to make certain the deadlines are met."*

- **How do you handle surprises that come up during the day?**
  - The interviewer wants to know if you get flustered when priorities change unexpectedly. When responding to this type of question focus on your flexibility.
  - **How to Say It:** *"Though I start each day with a set of priorities, there are occasions when pressing situations arise that need my immediate attention. In those cases, I reevaluate my to-do list and consolidate activities to accommodate urgent matters. I'm comfortable in unpredictable, high-paced environments and quickly adapt to last-minute challenges."*

- **Do you meet error-free deadlines?**
  - When answering this question, demonstrate that you are capable of completing projects on time, within the specified requirements, and error-free.
  - **How to Say It:** *"Before I begin a project, I make sure I understand the objective. Having a clear understanding of the goal allows me to delve into projects right away and reduces the chances of making mistakes."*

DECISION MAKING AND PROBLEM SOLVING

Interviewers will use the way you have made decisions or solved problems in the past as an indicator of your future successes. They want to know your track record for executing successful plans and learn how your decisions have affected departmental or organizational growth.

HOW TO SAY IT

- Be specific in your responses and use the foundation of storytelling—who, what, where, when, why. Who was involved in the process? What were the circumstances? Where was this accomplishment delivered? When was the accomplishment delivered? Why was the outcome important to the company? (See the STAR technique on page 89 for instructions on how to answer behavioral-style questions.)
- Craft responses that demonstrate you have the ability to anticipate problems and proactively resolve them.
- If asked a question about a situation that you don't have direct experience in, provide a response

focusing on what you would do if you were in that situation.

- If you don't have paid work experience when answering a performance-based question, use examples from volunteer activities or internships.

Power Words

achieved	executed	interpreted
adapted	expanded	led
applied	generated	researched
assessed	implemented	slashed
bolstered	improved	solved
delivered	integrated	spearheaded

Personal Characteristics

ambitious	goal driven	proficient
analytical	innovative	prudent
compelling	inquisitive	quick learner
conclusive	insightful	sensible
confident	levelheaded	shrewd
decisive	logical	sound
detailed	persuasive communicator	systematic
determined	practical	tenacious
dynamic	precise	thorough
efficient	productive	well-reasoned

Power Phrases

ability to shift perspectives quickly
analyze the facts quickly and make a decision
anticipate challenges in the early stages
believe all problems can be solved
carefully weigh all options
combine problem-solving techniques with creativity
consider long-range consequences
develop a sound plan for accomplishing goals
diplomatic problem solving
evaluate the effectiveness of the decision
examine the problem thoroughly, look at it from all angles
find a new perspective to resolve problems
follow up to ensure a plan is executed appropriately
identify the best outcome
made decisions that improved effectiveness
once I reach a decision, I follow through
pay attention to my gut instinct
proactive approach to decision making
provide a structure for working on the problem
put my decision into action
quickly identify the problem that needs to be addressed
recognize a problem and brainstorm ideas
see decisions through
sound decision maker
tackle situations with the end in mind
take accountability for my decisions, positive or negative
weigh options before making a final decision

Sample Decision Making and Problem Solving Interview Questions and Answers

- **What is the biggest challenge you faced within the last three months?**
  - When answering this question, provide a detailed response explaining what the challenge was and exactly how you resolved the issue. This is a time when the STAR technique on page 89 would be especially helpful.
  - **How to Say It:** *"Last month a client, the president of a publicly traded* Fortune *500 company, called to inform me that, as a cost-saving measure, the decision had been made to downsize the workforce. She was concerned about how to notify stockholders and investors. Given their financial stake in the company and the possibility that they would immediately sell their shares, both the delivery and the content of the message were critical. I wrote the presidential message, focusing on future plans to rebuild the organization. The message was well received by stakeholders, and the president received their commitment to support the organization through its difficult time."*
- **Tell me about a problem you took on. What was the result?**
  - Choose an example that had favorable results and showcases the skill sets that are most important for the position you are interviewing for.
  - **How to Say It:** *"At ABC Textiles, the manufacturing plant received numerous citations because it wasn't OSHA compliant. When I was promoted to site man-*

ager, I enrolled all supervisors for OSHA training. I then held a meeting with all the employees and stressed the importance of implementing safety measures. As a result, we haven't been fined by OSHA in nearly five years."

- **How will your problem-solving abilities benefit our organization?**
  - Focus your response on what you can offer that another candidate cannot. Don't hedge when answering this type of question. Be confident in your ability to positively affect the organization.
  - **How to Say It:** *"Throughout my management career in the technology sales arena, I have been successful in capitalizing on sales opportunities by securing value-driven partnerships, developing sales and marketing programs, and training team members in winning sales and account management strategies. You can be assured that I would bring this level of achievement to your organization."*
- **How much autonomy does your current or previous manager give you when solving a problem?**
  - The interviewer wants to know if your current or previous manager granted you the independence to tackle challenges on your own. When answering this question discuss your ability to make sound judgments.
  - **How to Say It:** *"I've proven my ability to be a natural problem solver who doesn't need oversight by succeeding in a number of projects. When I'm assigned a project, I'm provided the details and given the independence to come up with a viable plan of action in which to execute it.*

This works out really well because my manager can attend to her own priorities while knowing that I can be trusted to complete the project to her expectations."

- **Tell me about a time when you were challenged to reverse a negative situation.**
  - Give the interviewer an example of how you demonstrated an ability to thrive in a challenging situation.
  - **How to Say It:** *"The All Boys and Girls Mental Health Clinic had a well-publicized crisis in which the organization was accused of Medicaid fraud. The clinic received notice from the state, which outlined specific deficiencies to be addressed and resolved within one year or the facility would face a state shutdown. The director of the program recruited me to audit all clinical records and ensure compliance with state guidelines and proper treatment protocols. Through careful analysis of all records, I brought the clinic to compliance, and the organization was able to remain open without incident."*

CREATIVITY AND INNOVATION

Creativity is not reserved for artists. Anyone, in any field, can use creative skills when doing her job. In fact, an organization's competitive spirit is based on the creativity and innovation of its employees. This is the reason interviewers seek to recruit candidates who will take a proactive approach in developing and promoting the company's products and services.

HOW TO SAY IT

- Before the interview take the time to assess the direct effect your ideas have brought to your organization. Keep in mind that creative ideas come in small and big packages. For example, if you are an administrative assistant and you implemented a color-coded filing procedure that made it easier for clerical staff to locate records, remember that accomplishment has as much value as a sales manager who developed a plan that generated millions of dollars for a company.

Power Words

adopted
brainstormed
built
conceptualized
constructed
created
delivered
designed
developed
devised
executed
explored
headed
identified
implemented
improved
incorporated
instituted
introduced
invented
launched
manufactured
modified
reassessed
restructured
revitalized
shaped
strategized
streamlined
synthesized

Personal Characteristics

astute
attentive
conceptual
confident
creative
critical thinker
curious
go-getter
imaginative
industrious
insightful
intuitive

motivated
observant
open-minded
perceptive
persistent
problem-solver
reflective
resilient
resourceful
results driven
risk taker
self-starter
sharp
trailblazer
visionary

Power Phrases

challenge assumptions
challenge the status quo
contribute to companywide initiatives
develop lean, efficient solutions
devise solutions for improvement
evaluate and select the best idea
find alternative solutions
formulate effective strategies
generate ideas
implement successful solutions
improve production efficiency
introduce cutting-edge ideas
open to different options

Sample Creativity and Innovation Interview Questions and Answers

- **Would you characterize yourself as analytical or creative?**
    - Based on your profession, you should be aware whether the position requires a systematic or creative approach to problem solving. For example, if you are in accounting the interviewer will be looking for a candidate who is analytical. If you are in

marketing, the interviewer will be interested in the creative type. That said, most professions require both analytical and creative skills.

- **How to Say It:** *"I'm a little of both, depending on the situation. My creativity allows me to expand my thinking and come up with some really great alternatives to solve problems. And my analytical side allows me to step back and take a look at the ideas from a practical point of view."*

- **Tell me about a time you implemented a creative solution that received special recognition from management.**

    - To answer this question recall a time when an idea you developed saved a company time or money or in some way improved operations.
    - **How to Say It:** *"When I worked for Big Technology Solutions, I implemented a regional preventative maintenance program in which the facilities department spent its time servicing equipment instead of tending to it only when it wasn't functioning. This effort reduced overall repair costs by nine hundred thousand dollars annually. The program was so successful that it was adopted companywide."*
    - **How to Say It:** *"While at Smith, Jones & Associates, I noticed that some of the administrative assistants were overwhelmed with work but others didn't have much to do. I happened to be one of the administrative assistants who had extra time during the workday. I suggested that we implement a work share program in which we were able to distribute extra workloads. Management agreed, and the program worked very well. I received a letter of commendation from the office manager for my initiative."*

- **Describe your creative process.**
  - Everyone is going to have his own way of coming up with creative ideas, and the interviewer is simply interested in hearing about your approach.
  - **How to Say It:** *"As a creative person, I allow my mind to wander, never dismissing ideas that, at first blush, seem over the top. This open-mindedness allows me to weave unlikely ideas together to create an original, yet still functional plan."*

PRESENTATION SKILLS

Whether you are giving a presentation to coworkers, a single client, or to a group, interviewers will be looking for a new hire who is articulate, engaging, and persuasive. A well-organized presentation increases coworker buy-in, an organization's bottom line, and customer satisfaction. For this reason, interviewers are interested in how you present yourself.

HOW TO SAY IT

- To prepare for presentation skills interview questions, conduct the following preinterview exercises:
  - Identify the top three goals you wish to achieve when presenting and pinpoint how you successfully achieve your desired goals.
  - Consider how you prepare for a presentation to ensure it goes off without a hitch.

  - Take note of presentations you have given and recall how you engaged the audience or the listener.
  - Reflect on the best presentation you ever gave and mention the characteristics of the presentation that made it exceptional.

- Organizing your thoughts ahead of time will enable you to provide coherent and concise responses during the interview.
- Though it's important to be aware of your tone of voice and body language when answering any interview question, it's even more so when addressing questions regarding your presentation skills. For this reason, demonstrate confidence when answering interview questions and through your nonverbal communication.

Power Words

clarified	enlightened	presented
communicated	explained	related
connected	expressed	simplified
conveyed	influenced	stated
delivered	informed	touched
engaged	persuaded	updated

Personal Characteristics

articulate	charismatic	convincing
assertive	compelling	credible
appealing	competent	dynamic
believable	confident	effective communicator

eloquent
energetic
engaging
enthusiastic
expert
expressive
fascinating
impressive
interesting
inspiring
knowledgeable
likable
lively
memorable
motivational
moving
sharp
stimulating
thought-provoking
personable
persuasive
poised
polished
well-informed

Power Phrases

appeal to varied learning styles
clearly define the purpose of the presentation
connect with audience
convey message with confidence
craft a compelling message
create a memorable first impression
create a rapport with audience members
deal with questions appropriately
deliver concise presentations
deliver high-impact presentations
deliver powerful presentations, workshops, and seminars
deliver what I promise
encourage participation by asking open-ended questions
establish eye contact with the audience
hold the interest of the audience
keep the presentation focused
organize material in an effective manner
project and vary the tone of my voice
spark lively discussions
tailor presentation to the audience
use supporting materials effectively
use visual aids effectively

Sample Presentation Skills Interview Questions and Answers

- **How do you determine if a presentation was successful?**
    - Interviewers won't be looking for a specific answer here. When answering this type of question, reflect on presentations you have given in the past and think about what made them successful.
    - **How to Say It:** *"Delivering a strong presentation and getting the buyer interested in the products and services are important, but I found that the most telling part of the presentation is the follow-up. If participants linger after the presentation to ask questions, if they make a purchase, or they agree to set up a meeting, that is a sure-fire sign that the presentation was successful."*
- **What is the most important tool you use when presenting concepts to coworkers?**
    - To effectively answer this question, focus on the method you use (e.g., storytelling, encouragement of coworker participation, the use of props) to keep coworkers engaged in your presentation.
    - **How to Say It:** *"Since most of the information we take in is visual, I include graphics, pictures, and props in my presentations. Visuals act as reinforcements to my oral presentation, allowing coworkers to take in the ideas I am conveying."*

- **How do you manage a participant who is attempting to take over the presentation?**
  - Interviewers are aware that when presenting there is a likelihood that a heckler or know-it-all made his way into the room. When answering this type of question focus on your ability to remain calm when the unexpected happens instead of providing a blow-by-blow description of a specific situation.
  - **How to Say It:** *"I start every presentation describing the 'parking lot' method. By this I mean I inform participants ahead of time that if a question is asked that is out of the scope of the presentation, I will park it and write it on the flip chart. Then, at the end of the presentation, I will answer the question. This method works really well because participants know that they will be listened to and I will address all questions. Another effective way of handling a participant who is attempting to take over the presentation is by summarizing his or her view and moving on to the next talking point."*

- **What makes or breaks a presentation?**
  - With so many possible answers to this question—adapting one's communication style to the audience, delivering the presentation enthusiastically, or the use of visual aids—there isn't a right or wrong response. Simply provide your opinion, making sure to give a specific reason for your answer.
  - **How to Say It:** *"Preparation. Since the presentations I deliver represent my knowledge and the company I work for, I take great pride in developing informative*

and persuasive presentations that leave a positive, lasting impression."

- **How did you hone your presentation skills?**
  - While you may or may not have extensive presentation experience, you can still effectively answer this question by discussing any hands-on experience you have gained through college courses, work experiences, or specialized training.
  - **How to Say It:** *"I joined Speech Makers—an organization dedicated to developing the speaking skills of participants—and the organization has been a great resource for me since I have the opportunity to receive feedback on my presentation skills."*

- **In your opinion, where do most speakers fail?**
  - There are so many responses that can be given, including not reading the audience correctly and not being familiar with the material. Whatever your view, the interviewer is more interested in your explanation, so be sure to elaborate.
  - **How to Say It:** *"Most presenters use PowerPoint as a crutch. They create elaborate visual presentations and don't spend enough time creating strong, powerful messages. PowerPoint should complement the presentation, not be the focus. There is no substitute for compelling oral communication."*

- **Describe your sales presentation skills.**
  - A product doesn't sell itself. It is up to the sales person to deliver a message to the decision makers that is persuasive and consultative—those are the qualities an interviewer will be looking for.

- **How to Say It:** *"Before developing persuasive sales presentations, I conduct client assessments to ensure the presentation is geared to the specific needs of my audience. My presentations are interactive with a lot of audience participation to allow my clients to be engaged."*

10

Off-the-Wall Interview Questions

Ever since Microsoft decided to weed out overcoached candidates and differentiate among large pools of qualified applicants by asking off-the-wall interview questions, many companies have followed suit—making these questions standard interview practice for almost any industry or profession. Though Microsoft started the trend, interviewers have their own reasons for asking off-the-wall interview questions, including these:

- Seasoned HR professionals who have discovered a link between particular questions and performance on the job.
- Tough, aggressive managers who want to see the candidate's reaction and how he reasons through answers.
- Untrained employees who don't know what else to ask.

Because off-the-wall interview questions are impossible to predict, the only common characteristic they share is that they are zany in nature and may focus on learning about the following:

- Whether you are materialistic and driven by money at the expense of professional relationships. From the interviewer's point of view, employees motivated by riches may do whatever it takes to move up the corporate ladder, making the work environment uncomfortable and overcompetitive.
- Your character and personality traits and whether your transition will be smooth, without complications. Interviewers hire candidates who they can visualize working collaboratively with their peers.
- Whether you are a well-rounded, informed individual. This is because individuals who are knowledgeable in a variety of topics, including politics and pop culture, tend to be better conversationalists—an attribute that will come in handy when dealing with potential customers.
- Your ability to think creatively. This is an indispensable characteristic that will be useful when dealing with spur-of-the moment challenges.

Though the interview questions do have a specific purpose, some may seem personal and inappropriate. For example, you may be asked about your favorite pastime or hobbies. These types of questions may seem out of context and you may feel compelled to show annoyance, make faces, or comment unfavorably on the question or the interviewer. However, keep in mind that the interviewer is only attempting to try to get to know you better; he is not asking off-the-wall questions to discriminate against you regarding age, race, disability, religion, and/or place of birth. (See Chapter 12 for more information on how to handle inappropriate questions.)

HOW TO SAY IT

- Given that it is difficult to prepare for off-the-wall interview questions, keep your answers brief. The more you talk, the better the chance that you will put your foot in your mouth.
- Consider using humor to answer these questions. It can be an effective deflecting technique, especially for the ridiculous questions. However, gauge whether the interviewer wants a serious answer before using humor.
- It is highly recommended that you answer the questions posed. If you are truly offended by the question simply state, *"I'm uncomfortable answering that question without knowing the relevance to the open position. Can you please draw the connection for me?"* If you decide to do this, be aware that you will be running the risk of unnecessarily offending the interviewer since his intent was not to be offensive.

WHAT NOT TO SAY

- Don't be afraid of providing a wrong answer. It's better to provide a response than to say, *"I don't know."*
- Since the interviewer is simply testing your ability to think on your feet, most questions won't have a correct answer. For this reason, don't overthink your

response. But at the same token, steer away from providing a knee-jerk answer. Instead, take a moment or two to think. To buy time, repeat the question or ask the interviewer to rephrase it.

Personal Characteristics

clever	level headed	quick thinker
composed	imaginative	resourceful
creative	innovative	smart
critical thinker	poised	witty

Sample Off-the-Wall Interview Questions and Answers: Materialistic

- **Where did you go on your last vacation and where will you go on your next one?**
  - Most interviewers are looking for employees who are able to balance their personal and work lives. If you haven't been on a vacation in a long time, there is no need to start your response with, "*It's been ages since I've been on vacation.*" Instead, simply describe your last vacation.
  - **How to Say It:** "*On my last vacation I went to a wedding in Vermont. My good friends scheduled it during a long weekend, and I booked a great bed-and-breakfast and stayed for four days. It was celebratory, fun, and relaxing at the same time. My next vacation will be to go out West and have an active, outdoor trip.*"

- **If you won $25 million in the lottery, what would you do with the money?**
    - When answering this question consider the type of position you are applying for. For example, if you are in a conservative field such as finance, the interviewer may want to hear that you would invest the money. If you are in a creative field such as marketing, the interviewer may want to hear that you would use the money to go on a shopping spree.
    - **How to Say It:** *"On a personal level, I would talk to a few financial advisers and set goals that focus on improving not only my life but also the causes and charities that I value. As for my professional life, I would continue in the same field, but in a charitable venture."*

Sample Off-the-Wall Interview Questions and Answers: Character

- **What is the color of your car?**
    - This question isn't really about the color of your car—it is about your character traits. If you drive a red hot convertible, the interviewer may infer that you are creative and a risk-taker; if you drive a white Volkswagen, she may think you're a dependable and reliable employee. When answering this question, simply describe the color of your car. You can take it one step further by telling the interviewer the reason you purchased the car.
    - **How to Say It:** *"After a thoughtful search, I recently bought a white sports car with great mileage, a strong warranty, and a good dependability record."*

   - **How to Say It:** *"Since I like to take spur-of-the-moment driving trips, I purchased a red convertible so I can put the top down while I'm cruising the interstate."*

- **In a newspaper story written about your life, what would the headline say?**
   - When answering this question, choose an area of your life that you believe is important, unique, or special about you.
   - **How to Say It:** *"The headline would read: Welfare Kid Makes It to the Top. I am very proud of the fact that, although I grew up on public assistance, I always stayed focused, studied hard, and kept my eye on the prize. Fast forward to adulthood and I have an MBA and am about to embark on a successful career in international business."*

- **What would you do if you invented a device that could read people's minds?**
   - The interviewer might want to see how you would use something that could have a negative effect on society. When answering this question, focus your response on the good you would contribute to the community.
   - **How to Say It:** *"I wouldn't want to create a mind-reading machine for my personal use. I enjoy the process of figuring out mysteries on my own. I can, however, see that a mind-reading machine would be invaluable to those in law enforcement—perhaps even replacing the lie-detector test."*

Sample Off-the-Wall Interview Questions and Answers: Well Rounded

- **Imagine you could trade places with anyone for a week. The person could be famous or not famous, living or from history, real or fictional. With whom would you trade places and why?**
    - When answering this question, choose a figure that is middle-of-the-road so that you don't stir up negative emotions on behalf of the interviewer. For example, Rush Limbaugh and Howard Stern are polarizing. People either love them or hate them, and most likely you won't know the interviewer's point of view. It's safer to choose a person who is more neutral.
    - **How to Say It:** *"As I work my way up to management, I would like to learn from George Washington and discover how he was able to inspire and motivate those around him to work toward a common goal."*
- **What is your favorite television ad and why?**
    - The interviewer might want to see how much TV you watch and what kind of channels you watch (sports? gardening?) or to test your familiarity with social events. The interviewer might also want to see what you know about sales, marketing, or branding.
    - **How to Say It:** *"My favorite series of ads are the John Doe ones for Special Sports Shoes. I loved their Father's Day ad featuring John and the special bond he has with his father. The ads were well done, but not sappy. I also loved the one of John running in slow motion. He is a*

phenomenal athlete, a good person, and an excellent role model for the brand."

- **If you could get rid of one state in the United States, which one would it be?**
  - The interviewer might be curious to know how well traveled you are or if you've never left your own state. The interviewer might also want to see how well you know the country.
  - **How to Say It:** *"Since Rhode Island and Maryland are small states, I would merge each with a surrounding state."*

Sample Off-the-Wall Interview Questions and Answers: Creative

- **If you could be any animal, which one would it be and why?**
  - When answering this question, choose an animal that embodies the personal characteristics you'd like an employer to see in you.
  - **How to Say It:** *"I would be a dog because dogs are known to be loyal companions who are loved dearly by their owners."*
- **What do you prefer: an apple, an orange, or a banana?**
  - There is no right answer to this question. The interviewer is more interested in your logic rather than a specific response. For this reason, elaborate on your answer.

- **How to Say It:** *"I prefer a red apple because I associate the color red with passion, determination, and strength. It is a versatile fruit: It can be eaten as is to curb your appetite, added to other fruits for a refreshing salad, or baked into a pie to share with family and friends."*

- **If aliens landed on earth and offered you any position on their spaceship, what would you choose?**
  - This is a clever way to find out if you prefer to be in a leadership or supportive role. When answering this question, keep in mind the role you will have if hired for the position you are interviewing for.
  - **How to Say It:** *"I would want to be the pilot of the ship and be able to direct the ship to go anywhere I would want it to go. I'm sure the ship would be equipped with the latest, cutting-edge technology, and I thrive on learning new things."*

11

Discussing Career Challenges

The difference between a successful interview performance and an unproductive one is in your ability to keep your cool under any circumstance. One way to accomplish this is by not allowing career challenges to get the best of you when responding to questions that call attention to any previous employment struggles you may have had.

Here's the truth: When you are invited into an interview, the interviewer is already aware of your potential downfalls because she has read your résumé. But you were called into the interview regardless because the interviewer is hoping that you will say something during the interview that will make you worth the risk of hiring. This is precisely the reason you should address your challenges with confidence and no apologies.

This chapter covers the following common career challenges job seekers face:

- Employment gap
- Job hopper image

- Lack of experience
- Downsized professional

EMPLOYMENT GAP

With today's unpredictable economy, unemployment happens. A job search nowadays can take longer than it used to and employers are accustomed to interviewing candidates who have a gap. As a result, interviewers may make allowances for a less than stellar work history. That said, if you do have a gap, you shouldn't take it for granted that an interviewer will overlook it and you should prepare your response ahead of time.

HOW TO SAY IT

- An employment gap that is less than a year may pique the interest of the interviewer and he may briefly broach the subject but may not put a lot of weight on it since, for the most part, you've had a steady career progression.

  An employment gap that is more than a year will definitely raise questions for the interviewer. But keep in mind that from reviewing your résumé the interviewer is aware of the gap and decided to go ahead with the interview. If this is your situation, this means that your résumé left a positive impression on the interviewer so all is not lost. You can still come out on top.

  In either case, keep your response as short as possible so that you don't draw unnecessary attention to the gap. Instead, focus your answer on the skills, knowledge, and abilities you have to offer.

- Make use of the valuable skills you gained through nonemployment experience such as volunteer activities in your community.
- There are valid reasons for employment gaps such as taking time off to care for an elderly parent, a child, or to pursue a college education. If this is your situation, simply provide your response with no apologies and revert quickly to your enthusiasm for returning to the workforce.

WHAT NOT TO SAY

- A response such as caring for an elderly parent or taking a sabbatical is often unverifiable. And as tempting as it may be, don't mislead the interviewer with a false explanation. Choosing to fib may cause you to stumble through your response making it obvious that you are uncomfortable with your answer. Interviewers will pick up on your awkwardness and will quickly deduce that you are trying to hide something.

Power Words

available	reenter	return
bounce back	reestablish	revive
forge ahead	restore	start anew
rebound	resurrect	transform

Personal Characteristics

determined
enthusiastic
excited
geared up
pepped
positive outlook
willing
zealous

Power Phrases

completed relevant courses in the field
fully committed to becoming a valuable member of a results-focused team
maintained skill set through volunteerism
prepared to roll up my sleeves and get my hands dirty
ready to hit the ground running
ready to take on new challenges
recently brushed up on my skills
seeking to leverage my experience
stayed abreast of industry trends

Sample Employment Gap Interview Questions and Answers

- **What is the reason for your unemployment gap?**
  - From reading your résumé, the interviewer is aware of your unemployment gap and is interested in hearing your explanation. Without sounding apologetic, provide a response.
  - **How to Say It:** *"I've been on several interviews and have received job offers. Nevertheless, I take my career very seriously and instead of accepting a position I*

know isn't right for me, I am taking my time to find the perfect one."

- **How can we be sure your skills are up-to-date?**
  - Mention volunteer activities you participated in, classes you have taken, or temporary or part-time jobs you held during your hiatus that helped keep your skills fresh. If you haven't participated in any activities that kept your skills updated, focus on your enthusiasm to rejoin the workforce.
  - **How to Say It:** *"I've kept my skills up-to-date by working in temporary positions. From reading the job description posted online, I knew instantly that I'd be able to transfer all that I learned in accounts receivable and payable to assist your department in a full-time role. Now that we had the opportunity to talk at length regarding the responsibilities of the job, I am confident that I can make a contribution to your marketing department. This is exactly the opportunity I have been searching for."*
- **I see from your résumé that your last job was over a year ago in Las Vegas. Why did you decide to relocate?**
  - An employment gap coupled with a relocation makes interviewers nervous because they fear you may go back to your previous location. For this reason, your response should demonstrate that you are looking to return to the workforce and remain in your new location.
  - **How to Say It:** *"To be closer to our family, my wife and I decided to move to Chicago even though we did not have jobs lined up. This was a conscious decision on*

our part because we wanted to be sure the change in environment would fit with our long-term vision. Over the past year, we reacquainted ourselves with Chicago and decided on the location for our home. Now that we are officially settled, I'm back in the market."

- **Why did you decide to take a sabbatical?**
  - Sabbaticals are a time for rejuvenation and interviewers are aware of this. When answering this question talk about what you experienced and demonstrate enthusiasm for returning to your profession.
  - **How to Say It:** *"After a successful run as an art teacher, I decided to take a sabbatical and travel around the world visiting museums and taking a firsthand look at the work of famous artists, such as Monet, Picasso, and Kahlo. Now I'm ready to return to teaching and to share my valuable experiences with my students."*

JOB HOPPER IMAGE

What's the definition of a job hopper? The answer depends on who you are asking. Job hopping isn't considered a negative by some if the moves have been made to advance your career. On the other hand, if most of your job changes have been lateral, you may raise some eyebrows. Also, there are other considerations such as whether your industry is prone to a high turnover rate or if it's one that is easily affected by a sluggish economy.

Regardless of the reason for your choppy work history, the interviewer may be concerned about having to begin the recruiting process all over again soon after your hire. For this reason, it's important to demonstrate you are not a risk. Let's examine how you can overcome your job hopper image.

HOW TO SAY IT

- Before you begin the interview process, take a hard, honest look at the reason you have changed jobs frequently. Is the reason resolved? If it isn't, take the time to evaluate the core reason you are unsatisfied. Recognizing the root of the problem serves two purposes: (1) when you uncover the reason, you will be able to stop the cycle and find a satisfying career, and (2) you will be able to provide the interviewer with an honest, believable answer.
- Steer the conversation to the broad range of experiences and skills you developed throughout the years.
- Provide only the facts without going into unnecessary details regarding your frequent job changes. Keep your responses positive, refrain from negative comments, and focus your statements on the reasons you are interested in working for the hiring organization.

WHAT NOT TO SAY

- Your reaction is just as important as the words you use. Don't fidget, fiddle your thumbs, or look down when responding.
- Don't hem and haw before providing a response. Explain your situation without hesitation to demonstrate you are ready for a long-term position.

Power Words

ready
reassessed
reenergized
reexamined
refocused
reinvented
remain

Personal Characteristics

adaptable
flexible
independent
multitasker
open-minded
quick learner

Power Phrases

around for the long-haul
looking for stable employment
seeking a permanent position
settle down into a job for the long-term
transition to permanent employment
valuable learning experience

Sample Job Hopper Image Interview Questions and Answers

- **You've hopped from job to job. If hired, what guarantee do we have that you will remain with our company?**
  - The interviewer wants to be sure that you are prepared to make a commitment to the company. To answer this question effectively, you must

determine the reason you changed jobs frequently. Through this awareness, you will be able to stop the cycle and satisfy the interviewer's curiosity.

- **How to Say It:** *"My career dissatisfaction was due to the fact that I wasn't in a field that complemented my values. So I changed jobs quite frequently. After a lot of introspection, I realized that a career in the healthcare industry is where my values lie since I will be able to do what I enjoy most—care for those with physical limitations and developmental disabilities. Because of my newfound passion and the company research I conducted, I know that I will be happy here and be a contributing team member for a long time."*
- **How to Say It:** *"In the past, I accepted job offers without taking into consideration the direction of the hiring organization. This led me on the path to working for unstable companies whose revenues were decreasing year after year. Eventually, my positions were eliminated. Learning from my experiences, I now conduct thorough research on a company before submitting my résumé. From my research, it is obvious that your company is a stable one that has made great strides in the United States and is seeking to expand internationally. With my background as a business development specialist and your organization's plans to increase product visibility overseas, I am confident that we will have a long-term working relationship."*

- **What prompted your decision to leave the workforce to receive a college degree?**
  - Whether you always wanted to earn your degree and one day decided to take the plunge or you were passed over for promotions owing to your

lack of education, there isn't a right or wrong answer to this question. Simply tell the interviewer your reason.

- **How to Say It:** *"Because corporate America is now outsourcing data entry overseas, I spent the majority of last year working temporarily for several employers. I went back to school to receive a degree in business administration and am looking forward to working for an organization long-term."*

DOWNSIZED PROFESSIONAL

Was your position outsourced to a country where labor costs are one-third of what they are in the United States? Did management reduce its front-line staff while increasing executive bonuses? Did your position become redundant after a company merger?

Certain answers are considered standard, yet few people think about their responses ahead of time. When candidates are unprepared, their answers may showcase emotions that are valid but could be damaging to reveal during an interview. One of the most common interview questions is, *"Why are you currently in a job search?"* When you have been downsized and you need to communicate your situation to a hiring manager, your response should combine a positive reflection regarding your previous employer with a brief discussion of the business reasons you are no longer employed by that company.

HOW TO SAY IT

- Discuss your job loss in the general context of the company. Rather than personalizing the situation by saying, *"I was let go," "My job was eliminated,"* or *"My position was outsourced,"* discuss how a department or business group was eliminated. This demonstrates to the hiring manager that others lost their jobs as well and that the loss was not due to your individual performance. Sample scripts follow:

- *"A business decision was made to reduce the help desk staff by 50 percent."*
- *"As a result of a global company restructuring, the company reduced their New York workforce by 25 percent."*
- *"Due to global competition, the company closed its doors."*
- *"Due to the automation of our department, our positions were eliminated."*
- *"The accounting function was outsourced, and all ten accounting professionals were let go."*
- *"The marketing division was eliminated due to a new corporate direction."*
- *"Unfortunately my entire department of twenty was eliminated."*

- The interviewer wants to gauge if you are emotionally ready for employment. Before your interview, separate your emotions from the business reasons for a job loss. Practice your response and critique it. Do you personalize your situation or discuss it in a business context? Do your words flow? Do you sound sincere?

WHAT NOT TO SAY

- Don't show resentment through statements such as, *"I dedicated my life to the company and I received a pink slip after twenty years of service. My manager didn't tell me in person. I received notification in my paycheck envelope. I deserve to be treated better than that."*

Power Words

cutback	instability	recession
discharge	layoff	right size
downturn	outsource	volatility

Personal Characteristics

committed	loyal	reliable
cooperative	motivated	resilient
enthusiastic	positive	survivor

Power Phrases

affected by a slow economy
company closed due to lack of funding
corporate restructuring
decline in sales
downward spiral or streak
financial stress
forced sabbatical
loss of market share
organization shifted gears
plant closed due to a merger
store went out of business

Sample Downsized Professional Interview Questions and Answers

- **How many were in your department and how many were let go?**
  - The interviewer is trying to determine if the job loss was performance-based. When answering this question don't speculate as to the company or your manager's motives. Keep your responses focused on you and your positive experiences with the company.
  - **How to Say It:** *"The company suffered low fourth-quarter earnings, which translated into a 50 percent reduction of staff in four departments. In my group, the 50 percent reduction represented the elimination of six positions. The specific reasons for the decision were not communicated to me; however, I can assure you that the decision was not performance related. My manager was extremely satisfied with my performance and has offered to serve as a reference on my behalf."*
- **How do you feel about your previous employer's decision to downsize?**
  - When jobs are lost due to an executive decision to reduce costs, it's easy to become angry and feel betrayed by your former employer. If you allow this anger to come across in the interview, you will not be seen as the top candidate, even if you are the most qualified. Nobody wants to hire someone who's carrying around excess baggage or has a chip on his shoulder. Thus when answering this question, focus on what you liked about your previous

employer or what you learned while working for the company.

- **How to Say It:** *"I respect the organization's decision to downsize and hold no ill will. I was fortunate enough to be with New Tools Company for seven years. I had the opportunity to work with some exceptional programmers and hone my technical skills."*
- **How to Say It:** *"Throughout my employment with ABC Company, I was always treated well. My dedication and loyalty are underscored by my decision to remain with the company and help with the transition, whereas others in my department resigned immediately."*

Source: Barbara Safani, Career Solvers

LACK OF EXPERIENCE

Lack of experience doesn't necessarily hurt your chances of landing a job offer. This is because most hiring decisions are based on whether a candidate is likable and trainable, not on experience. Anyone can be taught the technical aspects of a job, but it is harder to train someone to be respectful, to have a strong work ethic, or to be a team player. For this reason, it is important to demonstrate your ability to get along with others and to adapt very quickly in new environments.

HOW TO SAY IT

- Steer the conversation to your soft skills such as organization, communication, and interpersonal skills and stress those during your interview.

- Make the most of your education, related hobbies, and the relevant work experience you gained through internships, volunteerism, or community organizations.
- Demonstrate enthusiasm for the position by asking a lot of questions regarding the company and its products or services.

WHAT NOT TO SAY

- Don't make desperate comments such as, *"Please all I need is a chance and I will be able to prove that I can do the job"* or *"No one wants to give me a chance."*
- Don't go into the interview with a defeatist attitude. If the interviewer has a strong sense that you are motivated, he will overlook your limited work experience.

Power Words

educated	knowledgeable	skilled
eligible	learned	suitable
hands-on	observed	well-versed
informed	qualified	willing

Personal Characteristics

ambitious	dependable	ethical
capable	determined	friendly
committed	doer	go-getter
competent	driven	hard worker

honest	responsible	talented
motivated	self-confident	tenacious
reliable	self-starter	worldly

Power Phrases

comprehensive field experience
gained experience through internships
nothing-is-impossible attitude
passion for growth and learning
possess strong interpersonal skills
quickly master new concepts
readily take on new challenges
sheer determination
solid academic background
take pride in a job well done
think quickly on my feet
thirst for knowledge
use common sense
willing to learn

Sample Lack of Experience Interview Questions and Answers

- **What have you learned in the one year you have been in the insurance industry?**
  - Take inventory of all that you accomplished. You will be surprised by the amount of knowledge you gained within a short time frame.
  - **How to Say It:** *"The one year of hands-on experience I have in the insurance industry provided me with comprehensive practice in automobile, home, and flood policies. As part of my daily responsibilities, I examined insurance claims to determine liability and communicated with policyholders to resolve discrepancies. These*

job-related skills can easily be transferred to your insurance firm."

- **Considering your lack of experience, why should I hire you?**
  - This is a question you should expect if you don't have the required job experience. When answering this question, determine the qualities you believe are important to an interviewer and focus your response around those issues.
  - **How to Say It:** *"What I lack in experience, I make up in communication and interpersonal skills. Let's face it: Anyone can be trained to create spreadsheets, but it is nearly impossible to train someone to work effectively with individuals and contribute to a productive work environment."*

- **How has your education prepared you for employment?**
  - Education can serve as valuable experience. When answering this type of question, make mention of your GPA if it is over a 3.5, internships, and/or any relevant courses you have taken.
  - **How to Say It:** *"My educational experience combined with my internship experiences has been excellent preparation for a journalism career. In my internship with the* New Town Gazette *at Jones & Sons, I used strong organizational, communication, and follow-through skills. I proved that I am able to work in deadline-driven environments while remaining calm when addressing crises. I achieved a reputation for consistently going beyond what was required."*

- **How to Say It:** *"In college I took classes in financial accounting, where I learned to interpret an organization's financial statements, and general accounting classes, where I learned accounting principles, including reconciling bank statements and payroll using Peachtree and QuickBooks. These courses have given me a strong accounting foundation, which I can easily build on for this position."*

- **With your limited work experience, why do you believe you qualify for our management trainee program?**
  - Management trainee programs are coveted positions, and companies invest time, money, and resources grooming the future leaders of their organizations. For this reason, you should emphasize your ambition and drive.
  - **How to Say It:** *"Though I'm new to the workforce, I'm no stranger to hard work. I enjoy environments that require learning new skills. I'm willing to start in an entry-level position and work my way up the corporate ladder. Through the combination of part-time, temporary, and seasonal jobs, I have developed a strong work ethic. With your organization's reputation for a strong management trainee program and my sincere desire to learn the ropes, we are a perfect match."*

12

Handling Inappropriate Interview Questions

If the question isn't job related, it shouldn't be asked. That is the mantra of most interviewers. Unfortunately, some interviewers may slip and ask questions regarding a candidate's age, race, disability, religion, and place of birth without giving thought to the inappropriateness of the question. How you choose to handle inappropriate interview questions is a personal decision, and this chapter includes options for you to consider.

HOW TO SAY IT

- If you are not offended by an inappropriate question and feel comfortable answering it, then do so without reservation.
- Use sound judgment when evaluating the inappropriateness of a question and don't automatically assume the worst. There may be times when the interviewer may ask an inappropriate question because it's a natural part of the conversation. For

example, if the interviewer is providing a tour of the facility and taking the time to explain company perks, he may discuss the onsite childcare facility. The interviewer might innocently ask if you have children. Though he can certainly go over company perks without inquiring about personal matters, the interviewer is most likely asking the question without malicious intent.

- Instead of answering the question outright, address the employer's unspoken concern. For example, if the interviewer asks about familial responsibilities, the concern may be that there will be constant interruptions in your workday. In a case such as this, an acceptable response would be, *"Throughout my career I have been successful in keeping my family life separate from my work life. I can assure you that I am committed to my career."* That reply is appropriate because you are not revealing information you would rather keep private, but you're homing in on the interviewer's fear—whether you can be counted on to fulfill the job requirements.
- Refuse to answer the question if you are truly offended or you feel that the employer has a hidden agenda. An appropriate response when presented with an inappropriate question is, *"Considering the responsibilities of the position, how does that question directly relate to the job description?"*

Power Words

applicable
inappropriate
improper
irrelevant
pertained
pertinent
provocative
related
suitable

Power Phrases

ask topical questions
beside the point
question is unrelated
remain on task
stick to relevant issues
uncomfortable with the question

Sample Inappropriate Interview Questions and Answers

- **Do you have children? Do you plan on having children?**
    - An interviewer may ask you this question to be certain you will be able to fulfill your job requirements and not be distracted by outside influences (chronic lateness, unavailable to work overtime, inability to travel).

    Straightforward Approach
    - **How to Say It:** *"No."*
    - **How to Say It:** *"Yes, I do. My children are all in college."*

    Address the Interviewer's Concern
    - **How to Say It:** *"At the moment, I am not planning on having children."*

- **How to Say It:** *"Yes, I do. Fortunately, my mother lives with us and she takes care of the children when my husband and I are working. Therefore, I'm available to work overtime when needed."*

Refuse to Answer the Question

- **How to Say It:** *"Let's bring the conversation back to the responsibilities of the job. What would you say is the most challenging aspect of the job?"*

More Information

- Though it is inappropriate for an interviewer to ask if you have or plan to have children, he can ask questions such as, *"Are you able to travel?"* and *"Are you able to begin work at seven a.m.?"* to determine your availability.
- If you do have children and need special accommodations, avoid answering the question by saying *"At this time, I prefer to keep my personal and business life separate,"* and revisit the subject when a firm offer is on the table and the negotiation process is in progress. (See Chapter 15 for information on negotiations.)

- **Do you practice a religion?**

  - The interviewer may inquire about religious affiliations because the organization is faith-based and she wants to make sure you will be comfortable in that type of environment. Or the position may require you to work overtime and/or on weekends and the interviewer wants to know if you have any religious obligations that would affect your availability.

Straightforward Approach

- **How to Say It:** *"Yes, I do."*

Address the Interviewer's Concern

- **How to Say It:** *"My faith will not impede on my ability to perform the job as specified by the job description. I am available to work overtime and on weekends."*
- **How to Say It:** *"I can assure you that I do not impose my religious beliefs on any individual."*

Refuse to Answer the Question

- **How to Say It:** *"This opportunity sounds very exciting and I look forward to participating in the rest of the interview process. If it's okay with you, I prefer to keep the conversation geared to issues relevant to the job."*

More Information

- An interviewer can ask, *"Are you comfortable working in a diverse organization?"* to determine if you are comfortable working with people of a different religion, culture, and/or race. In addition, she can ask, *"Are you available to work overtime?"* to make sure you can work the required hours.

• **How old are you?**

- The interviewer may ask this question because he is concerned that you lack experience or may be overqualified.

Straightforward Approach

- **How to Say It:** *"I'm thirty."*

- **How to Say It:** *"I'm in my early forties and have had great successes in the fifteen years I've been a consultant."*

Address the Interviewer's Concern

- **How to Say It:** *"I'm too young to retire but old enough to have secured valuable experience in this industry."*

Refuse to Answer the Question

- **How to Say It:** *"I'm sorry. I don't see the link between the question and the open position. Can you please rephrase the question?"*

More Information

- The interviewer can ask specific questions regarding your experience. For example, *"What type of experience do you have in marketing?"* and *"This is more of an entry-level position. With your strong background in finances, do you think you'll get bored easily?"* are appropriate questions.

- **Are you an American citizen?**

  - Interviewers may ask this question because they want to be sure you are eligible to work in the United States.

Straightforward Approach

- **How to Say It:** *"Yes."*

Address the Interviewer's Concern

- **How to Say It:** *"I am eligible to work in the United States."*

- **How to Say It:** *"No, and I'm searching for an organization who will sponsor an H-1B Visa. What is your company policy regarding this type of sponsorship?"*

More Information

- It is appropriate for an interviewer to ask, *"Are you eligible to work in the United States"* but not *"Are you an American citizen?"* This is because legal residents of the United States who have a green card or work visa are eligible to work in the United States, so a person's citizenship status is not actually relevant to his ability to legally take on a job.

- **Do you have any disabilities?**

  - The interviewer may ask this question because she wants to be certain you will be able to perform the job as outlined in the job description.

Straightforward Approach

- **How to Say It:** *"I am a picture of health."*
- **How to Say It:** *"I currently have carpal tunnel syndrome but have found that my typing skills aren't hindered when I have access to a special keyboard. In fact, I can type eighty-five words per minute."*

Address the Interviewer's Concern

- **How to Say It:** *"I don't have any physical limitations that will inhibit my ability to perform the job."*

Refuse to Answer the Question

- **How to Say It:** *"I'm uncomfortable answering the question since I'm unable to make the connection to* *how it pertains to the job. Can you please clarify it for me?"*

More Information

- The Americans with Disabilities Act allows interviewers to ask about your ability to perform a job, but not about your disabilities. Acceptable questions include the following: *"Can you lift fifty pounds?"* and *"This job requires employees be on their feet for up to six hours per day. Are you able to do that?"*

- **Have you ever been arrested?**

  - The interviewer may ask this question because he is concerned about theft or violence in the workplace.

Straightforward Approach

- **How to Say It:** *"No."*
- **How to Say It:** *"Yes"* (then offer an explanation).

Address the Interviewer's Concern

- **How to Say It:** *"I have never been convicted of a crime."*

Refuse to Answer the Question

- **How to Say It:** *"Since a candidate's arrest record cannot be used as a basis for hiring, let's discuss the issues that really matter. For example, I believe you will be quite interested in my experience in . . ."*

More Information

- It is appropriate to ask if you have been convicted of a crime on an application or during an interview, but asking if someone has been arrested is not the same and is actually inappropriate. Because an application doesn't leave enough room to offer detailed information, you may want to consider writing, "*Will discuss during interview*" on the application if you have been convicted of a crime. This will give you the opportunity to explain the circumstances surrounding the event. Remember, you don't have to divulge if you have been arrested but you are legally bound to disclose convictions.

The Finish Line

13

Questions to Ask During the Interview

Asking questions during the interview will ensure the meeting is a two-way conversation where both your needs and those of the interviewer are being met. This give-and-take approach will leave no room for unanswered questions or misunderstandings.

In addition to asking questions throughout the interview, you will be given the opportunity to ask questions at the end when the interviewer asks, *"Do you have any questions?"* In this case, all the effort you put into preparing for the interview can be overlooked if you stare blankly at the interviewer and respond with a *"no."* This is because in neglecting to ask questions, you may leave the interviewer with the impression that you aren't interested in the position or that you don't know enough about the company to ask meaningful questions. In either case, the interviewer may be put off and decide you aren't the right person for the job.

WHY ASKING QUESTIONS IS IMPORTANT

- Asking questions demonstrates that you take your career seriously and are willing to work for an organization only when there is a mutual fit.
- Developing well-thought-out questions will help you stand out from other candidates and allows the interviewer to gauge your interest in working for the organization.
- Passing on the chance to ask questions can be a costly mistake because it is a missed opportunity to learn more about the organization's culture, products, and services.

HOW TO SAY IT

- Allow the interviewer to answer questions fully before you jump in with another question.
- Ask for clarification when needed, but avoid asking the interviewer to reexplain an entire concept since doing so will give the impression you aren't paying close attention. Instead, paraphrase the interviewer's comments to make it clear that you'd like him or her to elaborate on a specific point. An example of a well-stated question is, *"I want to make sure I grasp exactly how the operating system functions. From my understanding, it's important for all the networks to be linked to ensure files can be retrieved from any computer in the office. Is that correct?"*
- You use judgment and time questions throughout the interview to steer the conversation in the right direction. For example, asking the question, *"What are the qualities you are looking for in a candidate?"* will

serve you best if asked in the beginning of the interview so you can formulate responses that home in on the interviewer's preferences right from the start.

- Start with questions that the interviewer can easily answer and save any controversial questions regarding the company's financial stability, downsizing, or outsourcing toward the end of the interview. These questions are fair game, and you should ask them; but it's best to do so when rapport has been built.
- Ask open-ended questions whenever possible because they require more than a yes or no response. For example, instead of asking, *"Did the previous employee resign?"* ask, *"Why is this position open?"* This gives the interviewer the opportunity to provide specifics.

WHAT NOT TO SAY

- Avoid asking what's-in-it-for-me-type questions too early in the interview process (questions surrounding salary, vacation, or benefits). The time to broach such topics is when a firm offer is on the table and you are in the middle of the negotiations process. (See Chapter 15 for more information on negotiating.)
- Don't ask questions that you should know the answers to, since it will imply that you didn't conduct proper research. For example, any answers that can be found on the company's website or brochure should not be asked.
- Don't ask questions that raise warning flags. For example, questions such as, *"Is it really necessary to work overtime?"* imply you do not have a strong work ethic.

- Although it is important for you to participate in the interview, don't monopolize the interview by asking question after question. Use your judgment and ask questions that are most important to you first. A good rule of thumb to follow is to limit your questions to three to five. Chances are that you will have more than one interview and can ask additional questions in a subsequent meeting.

FORMULATING JOB-SPECIFIC QUESTIONS

Determining questions you want to ask is an individual choice and no one question is better than another. That said, when developing questions, ask yourself, "*What do I need to know about the company to determine if this is the workplace for me?*" and formulate questions around those issues.

As a guide, you can use industry knowledge, online job descriptions, and corporate websites to determine what questions to ask. Following is information you can use to prepare questions in advance.

Industry Knowledge

- If you are a seasoned professional, you may already be aware of the issues that are important to you. For example, if you are an administrative assistant you may want to ask the following questions:
  - *"What personal errands will I be responsible for?"*
  - *"What kind of client interaction will I have?"*
  - *"Will I be required to travel to offsite meetings?"*

- If you are new to the field you can use the information you discovered during informational interviews to determine the appropriate questions to ask. Following are a couple of sample questions.
  - *"When I was speaking to Charles Wilson from ABC Company, he mentioned that your organization is expanding and you are looking for someone who can manage a multiline phone system. Is that accurate?"*
  - *In reviewing my accomplishments, Joan Herst, the CEO of Orange Electronics, noted that my qualifications in bid solicitation and quality assurance would be an asset to your purchasing department. Are there any other specific skills you are looking for in a new hire?"*

Online Job Descriptions

- Job descriptions have a wealth of information that you can use to easily create questions. For example, you can formulate the following questions from this job description:

  Coach, motivate, mentor, and train a sales team to boost sales. Incumbent should be skilled in growing client base, increasing company revenue and profits, and working closely with clients to establish long-term relationships.

  - *"Has the existing sales team met or exceeded goals?"*
  - *"What type of customer feedback does the sales force receive from clients regarding company products?"*
  - *"Can I have a copy of the sales brochure so I can review after the interview?"*
  - *"Will I have the opportunity to develop a sales-training program for the sales force?"*

Corporate Website

- Read through the company's website to learn about the organization you are interviewing with and develop questions surrounding the information you uncovered. Here are a couple of sample questions.
    - *"I noticed on your website that Management Associates owns Elite Properties and Global Homes—both of which are viable entities. Your organization has also made an investment in ABC Residential Properties. Has the investment met the organization's expectations?"*
    - *"In the profile posted on your company's website it mentions that your restaurant has more than eighty-three hundred locations. That is a very impressive number, and I am wondering if the corporation has plans to expand the market even further."*

Since you will have asked questions throughout the interview, you may be tempted to decline or say, *"You've already answered all my questions"* when asked if you have any questions at the end of the interview. Be aware, however, that your interest in the position is being evaluated, and you don't want to end the interview on an unimpressive note.

Take the time to develop ten to fifteen questions in advance. Having a selection to choose from will ensure you'll have questions to sprinkle throughout the interview and have three to five leftover to save for the end.

You should develop questions from a range of topics to keep the interview interesting. Make sure your questions are geared specifically to the screener, hiring manager, or executive recruiter because each person will have a different level of knowledge about the position and its technical requirements. To round out the interview, you can ask a question that brings the interview to a close.

QUESTIONS TO ASK IN A PHONE-SCREENING INTERVIEW

The questions you ask a screener can be general in nature and can focus on what you need to do to prepare for the "real" interview.

- **What is the name of the person (people) I will be meeting with?** This question may seem simple but it isn't rare for someone to go to an interview not having a clue who he will be interviewing with in the next round. In addition, asking this question will give you the opportunity to find out the type of interview you can expect so you can prepare ahead of time. For example, if you are told you will be meeting with the head of the department, you can expect a one-on-one interview. On the other hand, if you are told that you will be meeting with the head of the department, the lead supervisor, and a peer in the conference room, then you can expect a panel interview.
- **Can I please have directions to the office?** The worst thing you can do is arrive late to an interview because you got lost. Receiving directions in advance will give you the opportunity to do a dry run and make sure you know how to get to your destination.
- **Approximately how long will the interview last?** Whether you are interviewing during your lunch

hour or you schedule more than one interview in a day, you should know how long each interview will last so you can plan accordingly. Please keep in mind, however, that the time line provided will be only an estimate. It's best to ask for an extended lunch hour or to schedule plenty of time in between interviews to accommodate the actual length of the interview.

QUESTIONS TO ASK EXECUTIVE RECRUITERS

Treat a meeting with an executive recruiter like any other interview. Learn as much as you can about the recruiter's approach to placing candidates with potential employers and prepare questions that will help you learn as much about the hiring organization as you can before meeting with the potential employers.

- **Do you generally stay in touch with candidates and update them on the status of their applications?** Recruiters work for the hiring organization, not for you. For this reason, most are notorious for not returning candidate phone calls. Although recruiters don't work for you, they should still respect your time.
- **Have you sent other candidates on this assignment? If so, do you know the reasons a job offer wasn't extended?** The hiring organization usually provides recruiters with reasons a candidate wasn't selected. This is not proprietary information, so asking the recruiter to share it with you will help you learn more about the hiring organization's ideas for what makes an ideal candidate.

- **What can you tell me about the person who will be interviewing me?** Recruiters can serve as an information resource since they may be privy to the personality of the person you will be interviewing with and the type of questions she likes to ask. Armed with this knowledge, you will be able to prepare for the interview.
- **What is your niche in the marketplace?** Though it isn't necessary for a recruiter to specialize in a certain industry to be effective, those who do have intimate knowledge of the best and sometimes hidden opportunities in the market. This opens the door for you to interview with companies you may never have had the chance to meet with.
- **Why is the organization searching for a new . . .?** Recruiters have the inside track, and they will be able to tell you if the position has a high turnover rate, if it is a newly created position, or if the department is expanding. Knowing the reasons an organization is hiring can give you an indication of job security.

QUESTIONS TO ASK HIRING MANAGERS

An organization's management style can directly affect your job satisfaction. For this reason, it is important for you to get a grasp on how the department you will be working for is run.

- **Do you find that team members go the extra mile to ensure departmental goals are met?** Whether it's coming in early or working overtime or on the weekends, employees who feel valued go the extra mile to ensure the department is successful. On the other hand, unhappy employees become resentful and are reluctant to give more to the position than their job descriptions warrant. Asking this question will give you insight into the team's overall satisfaction with their department.

- **Can you describe the steps you take when a team member is not performing to the standards that are expected?** Your performance review isn't the time to discover that you fell short of meeting expectations. An effective manager is proactive and immediately offers coaching and constructive feedback to improve performance.
- **Can you describe the characteristics of a team member you enjoy managing?** The type of manager you inherit will heavily influence your level of satisfaction on the job, so it's important to learn as much as you can about his managing style. Does the manager prefer independent thinkers who take initiative? Or does he prefer micromanaging projects to ensure they're completed satisfactorily? These details will help you determine whether the work environment will fit well with the way you liked to be managed.
- **When departmental changes are being planned, are decisions made unilaterally or are staff members given the opportunity to provide their thoughts?** Some employees prefer to be part of the decision-making process, whereas others favor sitting by the sidelines. It's up to you to recognize which approach suits you best and determine which company can fulfill that need.
- **As a manager, how do you recognize the efforts of team members?** An effective manager realizes that

employee recognition—whether it is a pat on the back or a promotion—is directly related to employee morale. If feeling valued by your employer is important to you, the response to this question is important.

QUESTIONS TO LEARN MORE ABOUT THE INTERVIEWER

When asking interviewers questions, don't ask questions regarding personal matters—ask questions that directly relate to their position, the hiring organization, and the open position.

- **How has your position changed over the years?** As companies evolve, expand, or downsize, job descriptions may be altered to accommodate a new corporate direction. If the company is prone to add or eliminate tasks from job descriptions this is information you should be aware of.
- **Can you please tell me the reasons you decided to join XYZ Corporation? Has the organization met your expectations so far?** You can use the interviewer's satisfaction as a barometer. Chances are that if the organization met the interviewer's expectations then yours may be met as well.
- **Have you ever considered leaving the organization for another opportunity? If so, what were your reasons?** It is normal to have moments of discontentment on the job. But overall, interviewers should feel they are treated well, recognized for their efforts, and they are growing professionally.

QUESTIONS TO DISCOVER HOW THE COMPANY FUNCTIONS

Finding out the most you can about how companies function will be provide you with a sneak peak of their pros and cons. Armed with this information, you will be able to make an educated decision about whether the company is right for you.

- **Do you foresee any significant changes in XYZ Company?** Will new services and products be added? Is the department expanding? Will your job responsibilities change? You don't want to be caught in a bait-and-switch. By the end of the interview you should feel confident you will not be surprised by any major changes that could affect your position.
- **Are there any plans for a corporate merger or outsourcing initiatives?** When a merger or outsourcing happens, layoffs follow. Many candidates are under the misconception that only failing companies downsize. With today's global economy, no matter how stable an organization is, they are always tempted to cut costs or move jobs overseas.
- **What is the turnover rate for the company as a whole?** A high turnover rate can indicate internal challenges that haven't been properly addressed. On the flip side, if attrition is low you can assume morale is high and that the organization takes care of its employees.
- **Does your organization encourage employees to pursue additional education?** Progressive companies invest in their employees' professional development

since doing so benefits employees, customers, and the organization's bottom line. If education is important to you, knowing that the company will pay for such training will be of interest to you.

QUESTIONS REGARDING THE OPEN POSITION

The more you know about the open position, the better. Having a clear understanding of the position's history and what is expected of you will assist you in making an educated decision about whether you will be pleased with the job.

- **Why is this position open?** The response to this question will provide you with valuable information. For example, if the interviewer states that your predecessor was promoted, you can infer that the organization recognizes the efforts of its employees. If the interviewer reveals that the previous employee was not able to meet departmental objectives, then you can discuss the manager's expectations and how you can meet them.
- **I noticed this job posting has been open for a few months, so you've probably met with several candidates. Why hasn't a decision been made?** This is a good question to ask because you can use the interviewer's response to tailor your answers to their specific needs. For example, if the interviewer mentions the lack of customer service skills on the part of candidates, you can mention your ability to resolve customer concerns by clarifying their needs and determining the best solution.

- **Can you describe the employee you feel did the best job in this position? What made that person successful?** Did the ideal employee work late every night? Or did she work well in a team environment? The more information you learn regarding past employees, the easier it will be for you to mold your responses into what the employer is looking for.
- **What should be accomplished in the first three months in the position?** If the interviewer is able to provide a solid plan, it's a good indication that the company has specific goals set and that the department functions well. On the other hand, if the interviewer isn't able to provide a coherent answer, it may be an indication that the department is unstable—a fact you will want to know before you accept an offer.
- **In reviewing the job posting, I noticed the statement "other duties as assigned." Can you define some of those duties?** Will you be required to answer the phone when the receptionist is out to lunch? Or make coffee? Once you accept a job offer you do not want to be caught off guard by tasks you lack enthusiasm for. Asking for clarification on general statements made in a classified ad or job description will ensure you have all the information you need before making a decision.

BRINGING THE INTERVIEW TO A CLOSE

This is the final stretch. Anything you want to know regarding the company or its hiring practices that would affect your decision to take an offer should be asked at this point.

- **Now that you've had the time to learn more about my qualifications, how closely do they match the requirements for the open position?** Two things can happen when you ask this question. The first is that the interviewer can affirm that your experience, skills, and abilities are a perfect fit. Needless to say, if that is the interviewer's response, you have a good shot at landing a job offer. The second is that the interviewer may divulge that the company is looking to hire someone with more experience in one of your weak areas. If the latter occurs, you can use it as another opportunity to sell yourself.
- **How do I compare with the other candidates you have interviewed?** Finding out the strengths and weaknesses of your competition will allow you a chance to sell your qualifications to the interviewer.
- **I'm interested in the position. Have I provided all the information you need to extend a job offer?** Most candidates are qualified for the open position but fail to supply the interviewer with all the information needed to extend a job offer. This question opens the door for further dialogue on issues that need clarification.
- **Is there anything else I should know about the company or open position that will be useful to me?** Unwittingly, the interviewer may neglect to mention essential information regarding the position—information that could affect your decision in working for the organization.
- **May I follow up with you by phone or e-mail next week?** Following up after an interview is uncomfortable for job seekers because most believe that if the interviewer is interested she will call. The fact of

the matter is that if you take the initiative to call and inquire about the status of your application, you will stand out positively in the mind of the interviewer. (Read Chapter 14 for additional information on effective follow-up techniques.)

14

Effective Follow-Up Wins Job Offers

A surefire way to separate yourself from a sea of other qualified candidates is to write a follow-up letter after an interview. Most job seekers neglect to write a letter, assuming that once they leave the interviewer's office the interview is over. Well, it isn't. The interview process extends beyond the one-on-one meeting, and it is up to you to keep your candidacy in the forefront of the decision-maker's mind.

Candidates who follow up after an interview gain a competitive edge over those who don't because interviewers use the follow-up as a measurement of interest. Unfortunately, most candidates are reluctant to follow up for fear they won't prescribe to proper etiquette.

What many applicants don't realize is that the follow-up process is very flexible, and there are no hard-and-fast rules job seekers must follow. Each interview has its own dynamics and the follow-up process may be different for each. When you become familiar with the fundamentals, it will be almost impossible to fumble.

When following up, the best route to take is to write a follow-up letter first. If after sending a thank-you letter you don't receive a response, you can place a call to the interviewer.

FOLLOW-UP LETTERS

An initial follow-up letter should be sent within twenty-four hours after an interview. If you wait too long, an interviewer may assume you are not interested in the position and offer the job to someone else. You can choose to send one either through postal mail or through e-mail. The follow-up letter can be slanted to reflect your impression on how well the interview went:

- **Thanking the interviewer for the time taken to meet with you and for giving you the opportunity to learn more about the organization and the open position**. You should use this method when you are certain that the interview went very well and there aren't any pressing issues you need to address or clarify. This type of letter will most likely be short and sweet.
- **Reiterating your interest in the position and drawing parallels between what you have to offer and the organization's immediate needs.** Since you are elaborating on your qualifications and the requirements of the job, this type of follow-up letter will be longer than a simple thank-you note. You should use this method if you feel the interview went well, and you want to outline the reasons there is a perfect match between you and the company.
- **Addressing a concern that came up during the interview.** If you feel you didn't handle a question

appropriately or want to expand on an issue, use this type of note.

After the initial follow-up letter, you can choose to send another a week after for the following reasons:

- **Requesting a second interview so that you can resell your qualifications.** To entice the interviewer to give you a call, remind him or her of your most notable accomplishments. You should use this method if you didn't get a callback and want to remind the interviewer of your value.
- **Inquiring if a position you interviewed for is still open and if the interviewer needs additional information before making a final decision.** You should use this method if you haven't heard from the company and remain interested in the position.

Deciding whether to mail or e-mail a letter is a personal decision, but there are advantages and disadvantages to both.

Advantages

Follow-Up E-Mail

- Your follow-up letter will be received instantly. This will be especially helpful if the interviewer is making a quick hiring decision.
- You can clarify a sticking point immediately after the interview, so a negative situation cannot fester in the interviewer's mind.

Follow-Up Postal Letter

- Your letter is likely to end up in your applicant file, and when the interviewer is reviewing your

Quick Tip

There isn't a standard rule on how many times it's appropriate to follow up. You should go by your gut instinct. If your attempts go unanswered then it may be time to move on.

qualifications, the letter will serve as a reminder of your interest.

- If you want to address a specific topic at length, a follow-up letter is an appropriate format.

Disadvantages

Follow-Up E-Mail

- E-mails sometimes get lost in cyberspace or are mistakenly blocked by a spam filter. If the interviewer never responds you won't know if she received your message.
- E-mails tend to be short and sweet. If you want to clarify an issue, you may lose the reader's interest if your message is too long.
- The interviewer may delete your e-mail and not refer to it after the initial read.

Follow-Up Postal Letter

- If a hiring decision is scheduled to be made within three days, your letter may not arrive on time.
- The letter can get lost in the interviewer's overstuffed inbox, so she may not see it until a day or two after it arrives.

HOW TO SAY IT

- When interviewed by more than one person you should send an e-mail or mail a letter to each interviewer. This is because each interviewer has his or her own concerns and reasons for participating in the selection process. For example, a direct supervisor may be looking for a new hire who will make an immediate impact. On the other hand, a peer may be looking for someone with whom he can get along when participating in work activities. Having different audiences means that you can—and should—create different follow-up letters tailored to each interviewer's concerns.
- In an e-mail, the subject line should read, "Interview Follow Up" or "Thank You for the Interview."
- Whether e-mail or postal mail, use proper business practices when addressing the interviewer. For example, "Dear Mr. McBride" or "Dear Ms. Franks."
- In the opening paragraph, thank the interviewer for his time, include the date, and the job title you interviewed for. If you'd like, you can also include a brief statement about the company and your impression.
- In an e-mail, the body of the message should be one paragraph or two short paragraphs. In a postal letter, the body of the letter can be longer, but the letter shouldn't exceed one page. In either case, you can reiterate your interest in the position and persuade your potential employer that you are the right person for the job.
- In the closing paragraph, thank the interviewer, let him know you are available to answer additional questions, and that you are looking forward to a positive response.

WHAT NOT TO SAY

- When following up, the tone of your letter or e-mail should be professional and enthusiastic. Don't sound desperate or disenchanted that you haven't received a response.

FOLLOW-UP PHONE CALL

If after two weeks of sending a follow-up letter you don't hear back from the interviewer, call to inquire about the status of your application.

Advantages

- The interviewer may be more willing to discuss any concerns he has regarding your candidacy in a phone conversation rather than in an e-mail.
- You will have the benefit of hearing the interviewer's tone of voice and be able to decipher if he remains enthusiastic about your candidacy.

Disadvantages

- If you are annoyed by the interview process, your disenchantment may come across during the phone call and you may make defensive statements such as, *"It's been weeks and I haven't heard back regarding the open position,"* or by leaving a voice mail saying, *"This is my second phone call. Out of courtesy, I expect my phone call to be returned."* (See page 222 for sample follow-up telephone scripts.)
- You may catch the interviewer in an inopportune time and the conversation may not go as smoothly as you'd like.

HOW TO SAY IT

- When interviewed by more than one interviewer it isn't necessary to call everyone you spoke with. There will always be a person in charge of the hiring process, even if the hiring decision is a group effort. You need to place the call only to the leader.
- If you are having difficulty getting through to the interviewer during normal business hours, call before 9:00 a.m. or after 5:00 p.m. since it is more likely that the interviewer will pick up her own line before the workday begins or after the workday ends.
- It's acceptable to call the interviewer and ask why an offer wasn't extended by stating, *"I'd like to thank you for the opportunity to interview. As I continue my job search, I'm interested in learning how I can improve my interview skills. Would you mind sharing with me the areas I need to improve on?"* Focusing your question on your interview performance and not on the interviewer's decision not to hire you, will garner positive results.

  For this reason, refrain from making the interviewer uncomfortable by stating, *"Why didn't you offer me the position? I have the experience you were seeking. I just don't understand your reasoning."* Making such a statement will put the interviewer on the defensive and you will not receive the information you are seeking about how you can improve your chances of landing a job offer.

Power Words

recap
reiterate
restate
review
summarize
thank you

Power Phrases

appreciate your time
bring a wealth of knowledge
enjoyed interviewing with your company
enjoyed our discussion
excited by the prospect of working with you
ideal candidate
impressed by your staff
impressed with the offerings of your company
pleasure meeting you
reiterate my interest
remain interested in joining your team
thank you for the opportunity to interview
thank you for the tour of the facility
thank you for your consideration
the interview confirmed my interest
the position sounds both challenging and rewarding
would certainly enjoy working with you
you provided useful information

Sample Follow-up Letters

Quick E-Mail or Postal Mail Thank-You Letter

Dear (Courtesy) (Last Name):

Thank you for your time during my visit on Monday, January 25, when I interviewed for the customer service representative position. From our conversation, it was evident your organiza-

tion prides itself in establishing and maintaining positive, trusting relationships with customers.

Your company mission is in sync with my work ethic since I take great care in conducting thorough client needs assessments to provide top-notch service. This personal philosophy has contributed to my success in maintaining a strong client referral network from which we can both benefit.

Again, thank you. It was a pleasure meeting you and I remain interested in joining your team.

Sincerely,

(signature)
Bob Smith

Follow-Up E-Mail or Postal Mail Letter Offering Additional Information

Dear (Courtesy) (Last Name):

I appreciate the time you took out of your busy schedule to brief me on your company's need for an event planner. After our discussion, I realized we didn't touch on my experience in working in fast-paced environments.

When I worked for Reliable Solutions I was required to juggle a huge workload and concurrently manage numerous activities under strict time and budget stipulations. I was successful in meeting time, budget, and quality goals that earned across-the-board commendations.

What you will expect and get from me as a member of your team is dedication, enthusiasm, and professionalism. My previous employers can testify that I can be counted on to get the job done under difficult conditions and demanding schedules.

Thank you for your time and consideration. Please do not hesitate to contact me if I can answer any questions.
Sincerely,

(signature)
Barbara Cortes

Basic E-Mail Follow-Up or Thank-You Letter

Dear (Courtesy) (Last Name):
Thank you for taking the time to meet with me today. From our conversation, I understand your need for a team member who has strong accounts payable, accounts receivable, and payroll administration skills. With my comprehensive experience in these areas, I will be a valuable member of your team.

I look forward to your positive response. Feel free to e-mail me directly at frizvi@email.com should you have any questions.
Sincerely,

Furkhunda Rizvi
Phone: 555-555-5555
E-mail: frizvi@email.com

Follow-Up E-Mail or Postal Letter After a Rejection Letter

Dear (Courtesy) (Last Name):
I received your letter indicating that another candidate was chosen for the teaching position I interviewed for on March 21. Though I am disappointed I did not get the position, I value the time you took to meet with me.

If by chance the new hire doesn't meet your requirements or if there are future vacancies, please know that I remain interested in teaching for your district. Thank you for your time and consideration.

Sincerely,

(signature)
Claudia Martinez

Follow-Up Letter Requesting a Second Interview

Dear (Courtesy) (Last Name):

It is my understanding that the assistant clinical director position I interviewed for on April 23 has not been filled. I welcome an invitation for a second interview to further discuss my experience working with patients who have a broad range of physical, mental, and emotional conditions.

To refresh your memory, specific examples that illustrate my ability to do the job are:

- *As a clinical social worker for the Children and Family Center, I conducted psychotherapy sessions in individual, group, and family settings for special-needs patients while contributing to organizational growth through committee participation in the policy and procedure development.*
- *As a primary therapist with the Union Medical Center, I provided top-quality treatment and made progress with adolescents who were suffering from advanced psychiatric conditions.*
- *As a residential counselor with Mental Health Company, I worked with a group of adolescent females affected by emotional and behavioral disorders, using CPI methods to facilitate treatment and drive improvements.*

I would like to reiterate my strong interest in the position and in working with you and your staff. Please do not hesitate to contact me to set up a second interview. I can be reached at 555-555-5555.

Sincerely,

(signature)
Ross Martin

Follow-up Telephone Scripts

- *"Ms. Jones, this is a quick follow-up call to see if you have any questions regarding my qualifications. I remain interested in the position and am confident I can add value to your team."*
- *"Mr. Classy, thank you for taking my phone call. My enthusiasm for the position and interest were strengthened as a result of the information I received during our interview last week. Since time has passed, I'm calling to see if you have additional questions regarding my candidacy."*
- *"Mr. Chang, as you requested, I sent a list of references and writing samples for your review last week. I'm following up to see if you have additional questions or comments regarding my application."*
- *"Ms. Hirsch, thank you for sending me an e-mail updating me on the status of the customer service position I interviewed for last week. I understand that the position has been put on hold due to last-minute budget restrictions. I want to let you know that I remain interested in working for your organization and am available to start as soon the position becomes available. In the meantime, do you need additional information?"*

15

Negotiate an Attractive Compensation Package

Salary negotiations begin when your résumé lands on an interviewer's desk. Taking cues from your résumé—how it's written, your experience, and accomplishments—the interviewer will come up with a figure of your worth. Depending on your performance, you either confirm the interviewer's initial perception or the bar will be adjusted higher or lower.

Candidates often shy away from negotiating in fear that they will offend the interviewer, and the job offer will be rescinded, but that isn't the case. Most interviewers expect to negotiate and some can go as high as 20 percent above the initial offer. Whether the interviewer will budge depends on how you negotiate.

PREPARING FOR NEGOTIATIONS

To achieve favorable results you should prepare for negotiations before you embark on a job search. Knowing exactly what you need to live on and what perks are important to you will get you that much closer to a winning offer. To ensure negotiations run smoothly follow these four steps:

- **Create a budget.** Write down your monthly expenses to determine exactly what you need to make to live comfortably.
- **Determine your market.** Find out the going rate for your position and years of experience by asking recruiters, peers, and searching the Internet.
- **Prioritize.** Make a list of all your requirements and then divide them into three categories: must have, want, and would be nice. Items that fall into the must-have category are those that you aren't willing to compromise on (e.g., health benefits, retirement plan). Items that fall into the want category are those you are willing to give up in exchange for something else (e.g., not receiving moving expenses in exchange for a sign-on bonus), and the would-be-nice items are those that you can live without (e.g., office overlooking the city). (See page 226 for a list of negotiable items.)
- **Recognize your strengths and weaknesses.** What obstacles may you face during negotiations? Are you changing careers? Are you looking for significantly less or more than you have made in the past? Think of objections an interviewer may have and come up with ways to overcome his concerns.

Financial Analysis Form	
Housing Costs	
Mortgage or rent	$
Credit card payments	$
Electric	$
Phone	$
Water	$
Fuel gas or oil	$
Cable	$
Other	$
Automobile(s)	
Payment 1	$
Payment 2	$
Insurance	$
Gas/oil	$
Maintenance	$
Other	$
Insurance	
Homeowners	$
Auto	$
Life	$
Health	$
Disability	$
Incidentals	
Alimony	$
Child support	$
College loans	$
	Total =

Negotiable Items—Which Are Important to You?

	Must Have	Want	Would Be Nice
_____ Company car			
_____ Day-care services			
_____ Dental insurance			
_____ Desirable office			
_____ Disability insurance			
_____ Education and training programs			
_____ Expense accounts			
_____ Flexible schedule			
_____ Health insurance			
_____ Life insurance			
_____ Paid vacation			
_____ Paid sick leave			
_____ Paid holidays			
_____ Parking			
_____ Pension			
_____ Professional membership dues			
_____ Profit sharing			
_____ Relocation expenses			
_____ Sign-on bonus			
_____ Stock options			
_____ Severance pay			
_____ Tuition reimbursements			
_____ Unpaid leave time			
_____ 401(k)			

SALARY NEGOTIATION STYLES

When it comes to negotiating, it's all about the way you communicate your needs. If your emotions run high, everything can come crumbling down and offers can be rescinded. If you are too meek, you won't receive what you are entitled to. Recognizing and adapting your negotiation style can make a significant difference in the compensation package you end up with.

Aggressive Style

A candidate with an aggressive style enters negotiations with a clear understanding of his wants and may be less willing to compromise. This candidate may have a tendency to be confrontational and make statements such as, *"Come on, can't you do better than that?"* and *"I bring so much to the table. I can't believe this is what you are offering me."* To avoid making the negotiations uncomfortable, those with an aggressive style can do the following:

- View the negotiation process as a conversation and not as a game in which there is a winner and a loser.
- Keep in mind that the definition of a successful negotiation is when both parties are satisfied with the outcome.
- Don't personalize the negotiation process. Keep your tone conversational and nonemotional.
- Realize the negotiation process can take time. An agreement doesn't have to be reached in one meeting.

Passive Style

To avoid an uncomfortable situation, those with a passive negotiation style won't negotiate and will accept the first offer—even if the offer will put the company's needs ahead of their own. The result usually leaves the passive negotiator feeling shortchanged. To ensure a positive outcome, those with a passive negotiation style can do the following:

- Always ask the interviewer for twenty-four hours to collect your thoughts. You can use that time to decide how you will approach the interviewer with a counteroffer.
- Recognize that neither you nor the interviewer should feel shortchanged—the outcome should satisfy both parties.
- Realize that your salary should reflect your accomplishments, skills, and abilities.

Collaborative Style

Always looking for a solution that will work well for both parties, those with a collaborative style put equal weight on the company's point of view and their own needs. They take the time to consider alternatives and find a middle ground. By far, this is the most effective negotiation style.

HOW TO SAY IT

Fundamentals

- Organizations frown on candidates whose only interest is money. Allow the interview to run its natural course and hold off salary discussions until you've had the opportunity to showcase your qualifications. If you discuss salary too early, the following may happen:

  - The interviewer may question your interest in the position and conclude there isn't a fit.
  - You may overprice yourself and the interviewer may not extend an offer in fear they can't afford you.
  - Your salary request may be less than the interviewer had in mind, and he may question your ability to perform the job.

- Don't base your salary request on your current salary but rather on the responsibilities of the position you are interviewing for.
- When asked for salary requirements on an application write "open" or "negotiable." When asked about your previous salary write "will discuss during interview." *Note:* Providing inaccurate salary information on an application is a mistake since that information is easily verifiable by either contacting your previous employer or by running a credit check.
- Entry-level candidates have less negotiating power and for the most part can negotiate only salary. On the other hand, seasoned professionals are able to negotiate additional perks. (See page 226 for a list of negotiable items.)

Buying Time

- An offer that didn't seem acceptable at first blush may be appealing after you have given it some thought or vice versa. Because of this, ask for twenty-four hours to evaluate the pros and cons of the offer.
- If called with an offer you may want to consider requesting a face-to-face meeting. A sign that you should negotiate in person is if you are not pleased

with the terms and believe the negotiation process may be complicated. Negotiating in person will give you an advantage since you will be able to read the interviewer's nonverbal communication and make adjustments to your presentation accordingly.

Counteroffer

- Don't make a counteroffer just for negotiation's sake. Not all companies place a low-ball offer on the table. If you are offered a salary that meets your expectations, accept it.
- If the offer is unacceptable, don't decline it right away. Take the time to reassess the compensation package and pinpoint items you would like to negotiate.
- When presenting a counteroffer, be specific. What are you negotiating for? More money? Company perks? More paid time off? It's not enough to just state you are interested in additional benefits. Supply the interviewer with your exact needs. Don't frustrate the interviewer by making piece-meal requests. All items to be negotiated should be discussed upfront.

The Finish Line

- Refrain from negotiating once you have accepted the offer. The time to negotiate is before you agree to the terms.
- If you receive multiple job offers, don't put companies against each other. This strategy rarely works and gives the impression that you are basing your decision solely on compensation. Instead, take into

account all the factors each organization offers and base your decision on more than just salary. To assist you with the evaluation process and to choose a position that is the best overall fit for you, see the job evaluation chart on page 233.

ADDRESSING SALARY IN A COVER LETTER

You'll often notice that many job listings request that you include salary requirements in your cover letter to be considered for the position. Most applicants fear their candidacy will be eliminated, so they divulge their salary history. The truth is that fewer than 3 percent of hiring organizations that request salary histories in classified ads report disqualifying those who don't discuss salary in their cover letters.

Hiring organizations request salary for one reason: to screen out candidates who don't fall within the predetermined range. Some job seekers may argue that this isn't necessarily a negative. After all, if an organization can't meet your requirements, there isn't a reason to go through the motions of an interview. But the reality is that nothing is ever set in stone. Minds can be changed. The interviewer may be impressed by your qualifications and increase the offer or you may be willing to accept a lower offer because you are impressed by the company's offerings.

As a result, you have two options when it comes to addressing salary in a cover letter. You can either sidestep the request or meet it head-on. On the next page are sample statements you can include in your cover letter that address the salary question.

Statements Sidestepping Salary Requests

- *"The compensation package I seek is negotiable and I am prepared to discuss my requirements when given the opportunity to interview for this position."*
- *"In terms of salary, I am certain that your organization offers a fair compensation package."*
- *"My requirements are negotiable and depend on the job responsibilities and the benefits offered."*
- *"My salary requirements are negotiable, and I look forward to meeting with you in person to discuss the possibility of joining your team."*
- *"With your company's reputation for valuing its people, I am sure the salary range offered by ABC Company falls within the industry standards. I would appreciate the opportunity to set up a time to meet to discuss salary and my qualifications for the position."*

Statements Addressing Salary Requests Head-On

- *"Research suggests that the range for this position in an organization of your size is between thirty-five and forty-five thousand."*
- *"As you requested, my salary requirement is in the middle to high thirties."*
- *"Considering I am an outcome-driven professional with a winning approach to business development, I'm seeking a salary in the mid to upper sixties."*
- *"With my strong academic background, coupled with my work experience, I am requesting a salary of fifty-five thousand dollars plus 10 percent commission."*

Job Evaluation Checklist

	Job Offer 1	Job Offer 2	Job Offer 3
Job Satisfaction			
Desired job title			
Fits career goals			
Room for growth			
Hours			
Workweek hours			
Mandatory overtime			
Flextime			
Mutual Fit			
Management style			
Corporate culture			
Peer acceptance			
Desirable office			
Financial Considerations			
Acceptable salary			
Commission			
Sign-on bonus			
Annual raise			
Pension plan			
Tuition reimbursement			
Dental insurance			
Disability insurance			
Health insurance			
Life insurance			
Paid vacation			
Paid sick leave			
Paid holidays			
Stock options			
Severance pay			
Relocation expenses			
Perks			
Company car			
Day-care services			
Expense accounts			
Parking expenses			
Professional membership dues			
Country club dues			

NEGOTIATING WITH A HUMAN RESOURCES REPRESENTATIVE VS. THE HIRING MANAGER

Whether or not a company has a human resources department affects the negotiation process. This is because one of the human resources representative's primary responsibilities is to extend a job offer and participate in the negotiation process with candidates. Unfortunately, these representatives don't have the authority to make changes to the offer and must seek permission to make adjustments.

On the other hand, a company that doesn't have a human resources department allows you to negotiate with the hiring manger. This gives you an advantage because there is no middle person to deal with. You are talking directly to the decision-maker.

At the end of an interview, managers typically say, "Please call me if you have any questions." Make sure you do have questions to ask after the interview. Staying in touch with the hiring manager helps build rapport, shows your interest in the position, and gives you the all-important opportunity to negotiate directly with her when the time comes.

If you do receive the offer from a human resources person, in addition to thanking him for the offer, ask questions about other aspects of compensation *and* questions specific to the job. The HR person will probably not be able to answer those questions; thus you can ask to speak to the hiring manager directly. One big no-no: Do not try to go around the HR person. This will embarrass him and put you in a bad light with the organization. The HR person may not have the authority to change your offer but may be able to influence the hiring manager's decision. No sense making an enemy.

Source: Paul Munoz, HR Group, Inc.

WHEN A COMPROMISE CAN'T BE REACHED

- Be willing to walk away with no regrets. It is a mistake to accept a position when you are not fully satisfied with the terms. In the end, you will become resentful and begin to feel taken advantage of. That said, leave the lines of communication open. Circumstances can change, and what didn't work out during your initial negotiations, may work out later.
  - **How to Say It:** *"I'm sorry to see that a compromise couldn't be reached. This organization has a stellar reputation, and I am honored that an offer was extended. Should circumstances change, please know that I remain interested in the position."*
  - **How to Say It:** *"Thank you for the opportunity to interview for this position. I am sorry that we couldn't come to an agreement. May I contact you in six months and touch base? If the position is still open at that time, perhaps we can revisit the negotiations."*
  - **How to Say It:** *"This is a great organization to work for. Should another position open up that is in a higher salary grade, I would be interested in participating in the interview process."*
  - **How to Say It:** *"If the candidate that is hired for the position does not work out, please reconsider my application. I'd be willing to readdress the salary issue at a later time. Also, if the alternative candidate doesn't*

accept the job offer, I'd be willing to return to the negotiation table."

REJECTING A JOB OFFER

- There may be an occasion when you decide to decline an offer. In this case, call the interviewer. Don't send an e-mail or leave a voice mail. You want to leave the door open for future opportunities, and by not calling you may inadvertently offend the interviewer. Here are sample scripts:
  - **How to Say It:** *"Thank you for the opportunity to interview for your organization. I value the time you and your staff took to meet with me. After careful consideration, I've decided to accept a position with another organization."*
  - **How to Say It:** *"I regret to inform you that I have decided to accept another position. Your organization has a stellar reputation and I am grateful I had the opportunity to meet with you and discuss possibilities. I'm so impressed by your company and its offerings that I mentioned the opportunity to a colleague who had a successful thirteen-year run with ABC Company. She is well versed in marketing and sales and is a skilled negotiator and strategist. She'd be a perfect fit for your organization and falls into your salary range. Can she get in touch with you regarding this opportunity?"*
  - **How to Say It:** *"Thank you for taking the time to approach upper management with my concern regarding the pay scale for the position. I truly appreciate your efforts. Unfortunately, the salary of thirty-five thousand*

is well below what I expected and I have to decline your offer."

- **How to Say It:** *"I received and accepted another job offer this morning and unfortunately must decline your generous offer to join your team. Thank you for extending a job offer."*

Power Words

agreed
agreement
compromised
considered
dealt
happy medium
meet halfway
middle ground
negotiable
resolved
sign-on bonus
win-win

Power Phrases

consider fringe benefits
fair and equitable salary
negotiate a good package
reasonable counteroffer
total compensation package
willing to accept (consider) a fair offer
win-win outcome

Sample Negotiating Salary Questions and Answers

- **What are your salary requirements?**
  - This is a straightforward approach for asking your expected salary and can be presented at an interview or listed in a job application. You can reveal

your salary, provide a range, ask the interviewer what has been allocated for the position, or ask that salary discussions be held when you have a full understanding of the position. Your answer depends on which stage in the hiring process you're in at the time the question is asked.

Reveal Salary

- **How to Say It:** *"From my understanding, I will be reporting to the CFO and be responsible for the supervision of two accounting clerks. Is that correct?"* (Wait for response.) *"Considering the job requirements, I believe my salary should fall in the mid-nineties."*
- **How to Say It:** *"I'm looking for a salary in the neighborhood of seventy-five thousand dollars, depending on the benefits package."*

Hold Off Salary Discussions

- **How to Say It:** *"As of right now, I don't know enough about the position to provide a salary range. I'm sure that we will be able to come to an agreement once it's established there is a mutual fit."*
- **How to Say It:** *"I'd like to learn more about the organization and the job requirements before we discuss salary."*

Ask the Interviewer

- **How to Say It:** *"Considering the conversation we had today and the information provided on my résumé, what salary would you offer a candidate with my qualifications?"*
- **How to Say It:** *"What salary has been allocated for this position?"*

Provide a Range

- **How to Say It:** *"After conducting research, I have determined that the benchmark salary for a customer service representative with ten years of experience and a bachelor degree falls in the range of sixty to seventy-five thousand. Considering my accomplishments, I would fall in the higher end of that range."*

- **I'd like to offer you the position. We've allocated forty-five thousand dollars for this position. How does this sound to you?**

  - If the salary sounds fair, feel free to tell the interviewer. If it doesn't, then you should have your facts ready.

Accept the Terms

- **How to Say It:** *"I appreciate your company's fairness. I accept the offer."*

Buying Time

- **How to Say It:** *"That sounds like a fair and equitable offer. I'd like twenty-four hours to think about it. Can I get back to you by the end of tomorrow?"*

Asking for More

- **How to Say It:** *"I am very interested in the position. In researching salary requirements for a customer service manager with five years of experience, I noted the national average is sixty thousand dollars. Is there a way we could work this out?"*
- **How to Say It:** *"If you are able to offer an additional five thousand dollars, I'd be happy to accept your offer."*

Putting It on the Interviewer

- **How to Say It:** *"What was the ending salary of the person who previously held this position?"*
- **How to Say It:** *"The salary is lower than I expected. Is the offer negotiable?"*
- **How to Say It:** *"Your offer comes close to what I expected. Is the offer negotiable?"*
- **How to Say It:** *"The average salary for this type of position falls in the fifties. Is your offer negotiable?"*

- **The salary for this position is thirty-five thousand and is nonnegotiable.**
  - The interviewer may be this clear-cut because there is no wiggle room and he doesn't want to partake in salary negotiations.
  - **How to Say It:** *"Can I ask how the organization arrived at this figure? It's lower than I expected, but I remain interested in the position."*
  - **How to Say It:** *"Opportunities for growth exist here and I'm willing to consider a salary of thirty-five thousand, depending on the benefits offered by the company."*
  - **How to Say It:** *"The salary is lower than I expected. I understand that performance reviews are conducted every six months. Is it possible to receive a review in three months instead?"*

- **What exactly were you making with ABC Company?**
  - This is a sneaky way of getting you to reveal a number without making you feel as though you're in the negotiating processes.

- **How to Say It:** *"When I started with ABC Company my salary was sixty-three thousand. Throughout the six years I've worked for the company, I received annual performance-based raises. My current salary is seventy-eight thousand, and I naturally want to make more in my next position."*
- **How to Say It:** *"As you know, in my previous position my job title was assistant manager and the position I'm applying for is upper management. Considering the difference in responsibilities, I'm looking for an increase. What is the average starting salary for a manager in your company?"*

- **What is the minimum salary you will accept?**
  - Interviewers usually have a range in mind and they use your minimum requirements as a bargaining tool.
  - **How to Say It:** *"According to my research, the range for this position is twenty-three to twenty-eight thousand. Since I have three years of experience in managing customer accounts, I am looking for a salary on the higher end."*
  - **How to Say It:** *"In the past, I have made the mistake of accepting offers solely based on salary. After much reflection, I've realized that at this point in my career I am looking for an opportunity that complements my experience. Let's hold off on salary talks until we find out more about each other. How does that sound?"*

- **Why are you interested in working for us when the salary we offer is significantly less than what you are used to making?**

- This is a fair question. The interviewer wants to be sure that if you accept the position you won't regret accepting a lower salary and start looking for another opportunity soon after you're hired.
- **How to Say It:** *"I love being a manager, and the industry has changed drastically over the past few years. I realize that to stay in this industry, I have to take a cut in pay. I've made adjustments in my lifestyle to accommodate my new salary."*
- **How to Say It:** *"It is true that I was making more, but it is also true that I wasn't fulfilled. After much reflection, I realized that I would rather be working in an industry that pays less but that I find rewarding."*
- **How to Say It:** *"I am working seventy hours per week so the additional money I earn is a result of working overtime. Removing the overtime pay from the equation, the salary you are offering for a forty-hour workweek is comparable to my base salary. As I'm looking to cut down on overtime, the difference in salary won't be an issue."*

Sample Negotiating Extras and Perks Questions and Answers

- **Besides salary, what are the terms of your compensation package?**
  - The interviewer may ask this question because she knows that the company's salary range is below industry standards and is looking for a way to make the organization more attractive to you.

- **How to Say It:** *"As part of my compensation package, I request my moving expenses be covered."*
- **How to Say It:** *"Providing an allowance for travel to professional meetings* (or membership dues, country club, season tickets) *is an added benefit that would pique my interest."*
- **How to Say It:** *"Along with a sixty-five-thousand-dollar annual salary, I'd like the company to match my 401(k) contribution and pay the full amount of my health insurance premium."*

- **We would like you to join our team, but we can't meet your salary requirements. How can we make this work?**
  - Remember, almost anything is negotiable. Once you know the company is interested you can mention the extras you would like.
  - **How to Say It:** *"Due to my seniority with my current position, I am entitled to four weeks of vacation a year. If your organization is able to match my vacation time, I would like to join your team."*
  - **How to Say It:** *"In my last position, my ending salary was ninety-five thousand dollars. The offer of seventy-five falls below my expectations, but working for your organization continues to interest me. Can we come to an agreement of eighty-five thousand and a ten-thousand-dollar sign-on bonus?"*
  - **How to Say It:** *"I am a single mother and would like to see my children get on the school bus each morning. If my start time can begin at nine-thirty instead of nine, I'd be willing to consider your offer."*
  - **How to Say It:** *"Since a portion of my job requires me*

to sit behind a desk completing paperwork, I'm not needed onsite five days a week. Telecommunicating every Friday will allow me to save gas and toll money and that can offset the decrease in salary."

- **How to Say It:** *"Working in the city I always used public transportation to get to work. Moving to the suburbs will require me to purchase a car. If the company can lease a car for me that would make up the difference in pay."*
- **How to Say It:** *"I realize this is a start-up and I am excited about getting in on the ground floor. Should the complete funding not come through, I would like my separation agreement to include outplacement services."*

Get Your Offer In Writing

To avoid misunderstandings, especially if the negotiation process was complicated, make sure you receive an offer in writing that outlines the agreed-on terms. If the company fails to put the offer in writing then submit a letter of your own. Here is a sample:

Sample Acceptance Letter

Dear (Courtesy)(Last Name):

Thank you for offering me the position of marketing assistant with Royal Enterprises at the starting salary of $35,000 and a start date of October 26, 2007.

The following are the terms we agreed on:

- *Six sick days and two weeks' vacation per year*
- *401(k), with matching company funds*

- *80/20 health benefits coverage*
- *Performance review at the end of the probationary period*

I am confident I will be able to make an immediate contribution to the marketing department and look forward to joining your team.

Please let me know if you need additional information before my start date. As always, you can reach me at 555-555-5555.

Sincerely,

(signature)
Kelly Matos

Contributors

The following career coaches, résumé writers, and/or human resources consultants provided their expertise for this book.

Elaine Dreyer
Coaching Passages
www.CoachingPassages.com

Barbara Safani
Career Solvers
www.careersolvers.com

Paul Munoz
HR Group, Inc.

About the Author

Linda Matias, president of *Career*Strides (www.career strides.com), is recognized nationally as a career expert. She is in demand for her knowledge of the employment market, outplacement, job search strategies, interview preparation, and résumé writing. She has been cited as an expert in such publications as the *Wall Street Journal* and New York's *Newsday*.

In 2005, Linda developed and currently teaches a program for those interested in becoming a Certified Interview Coach (www.certifiedinterviewcoach.com). Specifically geared to training coaches on best interview practices, this is currently the only program that provides career professionals with a model they can use to coach job seekers in the interview process.

During her years in the career industry, Linda has coached and consulted with clients to establish their career directions, create powerful résumés, and improve their interview performances. In addition, she has earned credentials in all three primary aspects of the job search: Certified Interview Coach (CIC), Job and Career Transition Coach (JCTC), and Nationally Certified Résumé Writer (NCRW).

Linda is also the former president of the National Résumé Writers' Association. She writes a monthly online syndicated column that reaches more than five million readers per month. Topics include current hiring trends, creating winning résumés, strengthening interview performance, negotiating the offer, and launching successful job search campaigns.